Man,
Machines
and Tomorrow

By the same author

Engineering: An Outline for the Intending Student

Man, Machines and Tomorrow

M. W. Thring

Professor of Mechanical Engineering
Queen Mary College

with the assistance of

Avril Blake

Routledge and Kegan Paul
London and Boston

First published 1973
by Routledge and Kegan Paul Ltd
Broadway House, 68–74 Carter Lane
London EC4V 5EL and
9 Park Street, Boston, Mass. 02108, U.S.A.
Printed in Great Britain by
Ebenezer Baylis and Son Ltd
The Trinity Press, Worcester, and London
© M. W. Thring 1973

ISBN 0 7100 7555 3 (c)

Contents

Contents

Plates

Foreword by Lord Bowden

Professor Thring has written a book which might be held to be a gloss on the text that 'all organisms hold within themselves the seeds of their own decay'. He shows how the first Industrial Revolution enormously improved the standard of living of almost everyone in the world. Its achievements are spectacular in that, for example, the number of man-hours involved in spinning and processing an ounce of yarn has decreased tenfold every seventy years since Arkwright's time. It has in fact gone down a thousandfold in two hundred years, and the end is not in sight. This is the process which has made it possible for most people of the world to have reasonably cheap clothes, and it has done more than anything else to free them from the familiar vermin which have been their constant companions throughout most of recorded history.

The very success of the system is endangering its future and the future of mankind. If people have clothes cheaply, women are spared the delights of dressmaking and every shop-girl can follow the current fashion. This may be splendid, but it means that women have lost what used to be one of their more pleasurable activities. It is no longer necessary, many of them don't do it and they find themselves bored in consequence.

There once was a time when most people had to walk across the countryside if they wanted to go anywhere on business and it is astonishing how many people used to wander about Europe on foot in the middle ages. Nowadays people can fly easily and half the pleasure of travel has been lost. Furthermore, enormous areas of the countryside have been devastated by aerodromes and people all over the world are deafened by the noise the planes make.

It is perfectly obvious that we have lost our way and that if the system which created modern society is not to destroy it, then it needs to change fundamentally and radically. Hitherto we have always assumed that the policy of industry should be guided by the profits it earned and the public interest has all too often been forgotten. If the efforts of modern engineers were suitably directed, they could restore the environment and improve furthermore the lives of handicapped people, old people and people who are simply bored.

Professor Thring has discussed some of the possibilities of the new machinery and of the new society which they might help to create. His book should give us cause for hope. The book should be read by politicians, for it is they who will decide how our engineers are to occupy themselves, and what they do for mankind. An enlightened public opinion must inspire the politicians and this book may help to create it.

This book indicates the way in which we must make much more intelligent use of the powers given to us by engineers if we are to avoid machines causing a catastrophic decline in the quality of our life. Machines must be put in the position of being our slaves instead of our masters, as they are rapidly becoming. The machines of the first Industrial Revolution have increased production from an hour's work on a farm or in a factory by a factor of the order of ten and this has given a majority of people in the developed countries a good standard of living. However, it is becoming clear that further development of the profit-orientated growth economy will lead to an 'affluent society' in which the quality of life in the developed countries will steadily deteriorate while that in the undeveloped countries will remain low, for the following reasons:

(1) No government of a rich country is succeeding in finding a way of giving the less developed countries the benefits of the first Industrial Revolution. This is a cause of world tension and guilt.

(2) The success of the engineer in increasing the destructive power of weapons causes everyone to live in fear of another world war.

(3) Chemical pollution of air, water, sea and land is an increasing consequence of cheap engineering. It costs too much to clean out the pollutants.

(4) Noise, accidents, ugliness, and crowding steadily increase the stress on people.

(5) The opportunity for craftsmanship and achievement in daily work is steadily removed by mass production and mechanization and replaced by repetitive unskilled operations.

(6) It is certain that further increases in production per man-hour resulting from automation cannot be fully absorbed by a further increase in purchase of new types of consumer goods because of (a) limitations of space and raw materials especially fuel, and (b) rising

consumer resistance to the accumulation of more devices. This means an inevitable steady rise in unemployment.

It is the machines made by the engineer that are being allowed to destroy the quality of life in these ways. I therefore maintain that it is the engineer who must devise the machines that can serve as the slaves of mankind to give a maximum quality of life to all humans. I take as the crucial date by which the choice must be made, the year 2000. If no catastrophe of world war or epidemic intervenes there will be 7,000 million people in the world by that date.

It is the theme of this book that even in a world with 7,000 million people and limited resources of air, water, land and fuels, it is possible for every human being to live a life of considerably better quality than he lives at present. This implies a new basic motivation of society – the need for the individual to find self-fulfilment through creative achievement of value to others would have to take priority over the desire of the individual for more consumer goods. In such a Creative Society the quality of life could be high because everyone would be able to find self-fulfilment even though the standard of living is necessarily limited by the limitation of world resources.

The book discusses the machines that the engineer must develop if we are to avoid all the defects of the affluent society. At present it is much easier to get money to develop new war machines or super-sonic planes than to get money to develop medical, educational and other machines for service to the individual. In the Creative Society priority would be given to the needs of the individual so that human service engineering could make strides comparable to those of rocketry in the present era. Aids to diagnosis as vital as X-rays would enable any defect inside the body to be diagnosed without surgery, while artificial organs and nerve control systems for paralysed limbs will be developed. High priority given to machines to help education and communication could break down all the barriers that divide mankind into mutually antagonistic groups.

Once the idea is accepted that a man or woman judges their success in life by their creative achievements rather than by having a larger car than other people, it becomes possible to give everyone a fully adequate standard of living and to develop machines that enable this to be produced without anyone doing dangerous, uncomfortable or boring work. Coal can be mined without people going underground, work at the bottom of the sea can be done by machines controlled by people on the ground, and all boring repetitive work can be done by robots. However, these machines will reduce the hours of work required to earn a living and in the Creative Society everyone will have a right to a proper job – it follows that factory work will be rationed (at about half the present working life) and that a much higher proportion of people will work on human service and agricultural activities than in the present developed communities.

Non-polluting, fuel-economizing public transport systems will be developed to give everyone in the world reasonable opportunities for local and intercontinental travel at optimum speeds without the discomforts and delays of present systems. The engineer can solve all the problems of providing the less developed countries with an optimum standard of living and life conditions once he gives his mind to it, uninhibited by the luxurious and extravagant objectives to which the developed countries have been conditioned by advertising and political systems promising pie in the sky.

The book tries to establish the possibility of a real machine-served society in which all men and women are free to find their self-fulfilment to the limit of their possibilities.

1

Suicide or Survival

There is an inventor in all of us. Man, *homo sapiens*, is genetically curious, adaptive and exploratory. He will explore for exploring's sake and seek the solution of a problem because the problem is there. The inventor, the researcher, uses his imagination in the same way as the artist. To achieve his best work, he may well have to suffer the same agony of mind and need the same singleness of purpose to reach success. Success, too, when it comes, holds the same sense of self-fulfilment – a pleasure, pride and peace that has a true value no matter what turmoil of change is affecting other aspects of the inventor's life.

We are all living through a period of turmoil. This has been analysed by many writers. Alvin Toffler, for example, in his book, *Future Shock* (Bodley Head, 1970), has written: '. . . a growing body of reputable opinion asserts that the present movement represents nothing less than the second great divide in human history, comparable in magnitude only with that first great break in historic continuity, the shift from barbarism to civilisation.' He speaks of 'dizzying disorientation' and fears that 'The malaise, mass neurosis and free floating violence already apparent in contemporary life are merely a foretaste of what may lie ahead unless we come to understand and treat this disease.'

I, myself, believe that no pace of change would cause 'dizzying disorientation' if people felt their progress to be in the right direction: that is to say a direction natural to human beings in satisfying their inbuilt idealism, their 'onward-upward' urge. I feel that the 'malaise, mass neurosis and free floating violence' have come about because we have only used our new technology to give us a self-indulgent 'one up on the Jones's' way of life. This, as we are proving, does not work. What our Victorian ancestors used to call 'the Primrose Path' seems pleasant and easy to tread at its beginning and at first even leads to actual happiness in its contrast with the straitened and narrow life many of us had led before, but after a while pleasure in possessions reaches a saturation point and there is disillusionment. I believe we have, in the industrially developed countries, collectively reached this point. Therefore, it is time to try a new path. The question is – which path should we take? We seem to be at a crossroads.

The older generation tend to want to go back along the way we have come to find the pattern of living that was 'conventional' in their own youth; but a great deal of good as well as bad has come with the 'permissive society' and the 'meritocracy' and no one would really want this good to be lost.

At the other extreme, the more fanatical among the young want to destroy all that remains of 'establishment' order and start again with a clean slate. The young anarchists' ideas, after destruction, however, tend to be less well defined and anyone who has lived through a world war, or even studied the history of violent revolutions, has learned that destruction for its own sake is only retrogressive. We need constructive planning, not destruction or nostalgia. Fanaticism and dreams have never solved anything. We need to keep our feet on the firm ground of practicality and moderation.

In these circumstances, it seems to me that an engineer may put forward as valid a solution as anyone to some of the world's problems. Engineers are, after all, essentially practical and moderate men. They have to be. Their ideas have to be made to work in socially and financially realistic terms. The steam engine was in operation long before the laws of thermodynamics were defined as a theory. Engineers have to think 'with their hands', and in three dimensions. However beautiful the draughtsmanship of a working drawing, it is no use at all unless the object it depicts works 'in the round'. Unless an invention can be marketed at a price the majority of its potential users can afford, then it will have failed its purpose as surely as if it had failed to work mechanically. Yet the most technically and economically practical solutions will have also, desirably, aesthetic beauty and social value. Furthermore, the inventor's ideas may change the whole world's way of living, so that he must think 'in the round', too, in terms of responsibility.

In this book I want to begin by looking briefly at the great

1 Viewphone, developed by Prowest Electronics with industrial design by Butler/Isherwood/Bartlett as part of a feasibility study for the British Post Office. The chassis is a square ring of diecast aluminium which takes the weight of the fixed-focus camera/monitor combination and acts as a heat sink.

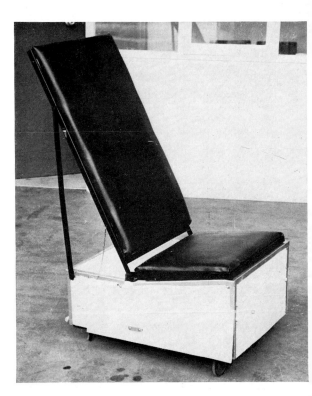

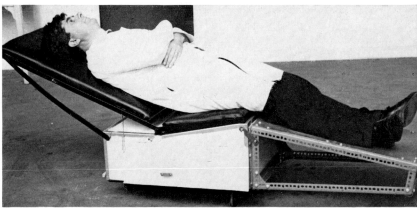

2a (above) Mock-up of the trolley-seat for a proposed international transportation system. The passenger would take his seat with him from starting-point to destination, since it is designed to be pushed by hand or to be locked into position on individual power units, or in buses, trains and aircraft.

2b (below) The trolley-seat in a reclining position to allow passengers to sleep on long journeys. Luggage would be stored under the seat and in the wedge-shaped unit that acts as a foot-rest or can be stowed behind the seat-back.

achievements of engineers and scientists, particularly over the past two centuries, and to assess their work in so far as it has helped or threatened mankind. No one would belittle the enormous benefits technology and medicine have brought us. Discovery upon discovery has eased mankind's lot and lengthened our life-span: yet the whole world stands under the threefold threat of destruction by nuclear war, by famine or by the poisoning of our natural environment.

R. Buckminster Fuller has written (*Utopia or Oblivion*, Bantam Books, 1969; Allen Lane, 1970): 'So I'll say to you that man on earth is now clearly faced with the choice of Utopia or Oblivion. If he chooses the latter, he can go right on leaving his fate to his political leaders. If, however, he chooses Utopia, he must get busy very fast.'

To me, also, speed seems essential. Charles A. Reich, in *The Greening of America* (Random House, 1970; Allen Lane, 1971), has seen our salvation in education – formal education and education through the media – which will create a climate of consciousness that may eventually inspire people to persuade their politicians to cure the world's ills. I agree that education is the long-term answer, but I think we need to take more positive and immediate action as well. The quality of life for the individual living in the industrially developed countries is already arguably lower than it was at the beginning of the century. What many have gained in social freedom we have all lost in noise, dirt, monotony in our work, lack of purpose in living and any close relationship with natural things. Also, this quality in our way of living is becoming progressively less high. We poison our environment daily to the point where, if we go on as we are going, life in our cities will become intolerable before the end of the century – if we survive so long.

Only a scientist can know how imminent is the danger of destruction – in the first place, by pollution, although hunger could follow and be followed, in its turn, by war. In reaching a saturation point in the demand for possessions, we are already facing unemployment. This could rise to 50 per cent of the population by the year 2000. Fifty per cent of all people could then feel degraded, discontented and anxious – and be, therefore, easily roused to find a solution in war. And this could become fact even in the wealthy, industrially developed countries. In the under-developed countries, the help given at the present time is worse than useless because it is operated either by businessmen out to make a profit, or else by power-blocks competing

B

with each other. The result is that the rich get richer and the poor get poorer, with the consequent spread of starvation and misery.

Unless we can change the world's social motives and build a society that rations paid work, that educates to give everyone a chance to feel valuable and self-fulfilled in his community, that reorganizes the world's food supplies to wipe out malnutrition, then deterioration will begin and lead to want and then to war – and we all know that war now means total annihilation.

So we must act, if we are to survive. We are already acting, particularly by teaching. The young of this generation, educated, do have ideals, but it will be a long time before they are experienced enough to win real power. It is up to an older generation to lead them, and I would like to put forward the idea that perhaps engineers and scientists might be good people to make a start in this. Since we brought to the world the inventions that have created the dilemma, we might set our record straight by being the people to find a way out of it. Engineers alone, after all, can foresee and make the machines that a new type of social system would need. Scientists alone know how to go about such diverse practical questions as reorganizing food supplies, finding the causes and cures of pollution and harnessing natural resources. Also, we already form an international community. We already get together and talk about these things.

Our main difficulty in helping the rest of the world, however, may be that of communication. In general, historically, we engineers and scientists have tended to become intellectually isolated from our contemporaries who deal in the arts and humanities. Talking among ourselves through mathematics and the jargon of our specialist subjects, it may not be easy for us to state our ideas clearly and comprehensibly to people whose minds have been trained to other disciplines. Yet I believe we must do this and that such an exchange of information is an essential part of any final plan for mankind's survival. All men, everywhere, must exchange information and work out a formula for future living that will allow us to gain the full benefit from invention without its present counterbalancing dangers. Psychologists tell us that the most powerful urges in human beings are the creative urge and the destructive urge, but I am optimist enough to think that our collective life-wish is stronger than our death-wish and that, if we can all work together, we shall, with luck, save ourselves yet.

4

Fear has divided us in the past. Fear should now bring us together. Fear may cause us, even as individuals, either to shrink away or else to become aggressive: we may 'lose' from an encounter or make the other person 'feel small'. If we can break down the barriers of fear and begin to exchange ideas on a person-to-person basis, we shall all grow and not shrink; but, just as we need freedom from fear in order to improve social conditions, to achieve this absence of fear social conditions must be made right. We must be freed, as soon as possible, from the basic anxieties of having insufficient food, shelter and warmth. We must have reasonable transport facilities, education and medical services. Economic expansion, a wealth-orientated society, will remain necessary if an ever increasing percentage of the world's population is to enjoy this basic security of home, health and food.

It is only after that point that the quest for material wealth, as an end in itself, ceases to bring any lasting sense of satisfaction, either to the individual or the community. Two hundred years ago, when the only power available was that of the horse, the ox, the ass, the wind or the water and all our clothes and consumer goods were made by men's hands, using only hand tools, no one spoke of life as 'a rat race'. In fact it is worth a second look at the British way of life as it was at the height, and end, of the land/wealth-based society in the middle of the eighteenth century.

G. M. Trevelyan tells us in *British History in the Nineteenth Century and After* and in *English Social History* (Longman, 1922 and 1942): 'Village life embraced the chief daily concerns of the majority of Englishmen . . . not then a moribund society' but with 'a considerable measure of equality and independence . . . The wives and families of the yeomen and agricultural labourers and the labourers themselves when fieldwork was slack carried on various branches of manufacture in their own cottages . . . The smaller country houses contained all the year round the homelier squires . . . In country houses, great and small, life was lived at its fullest. The zeal for estate management and agricultural improvement took the squire out on his horse at all hours of the day and the ladies at home' had 'for weeks and months together large parties of visitors' to be 'entertained with much eating and drinking, with field sports, with music and literature, with cards and dice'.

'Perhaps,' says Trevelyan of the aristocracy of this period, 'no set of men and women since the world began enjoyed so many different sides of life, with so much zest.'

No one would want to return to social élitism, yet surely there were qualities in this way of living which, restored, might help us combat the 'malaise, mass neurosis and free floating violence'. There was, for instance, a fundamental security for everyone in belonging to a community; a mental stimulus in having variety in daily work; a creative pride in doing skilled work with one's hands; a benefit to health in working out of doors as well as in; companionship in sharing cultural interests; and, above all, the success of this formula is proved by the fact that there was, as Trevelyan states, a prevailing *zest for living*.

The need now is to regain the sense of pleasure and purpose in life without one set of people, anywhere in the world, being the servers, the 'have nots', while others are the served, the 'haves'. Progress at this point in history must be intentionally for everyone, world-wide, although the economic practicalities of the last two hundred years have led to there being an *avant-garde*, who may well be reaping the tares as well as the wheat of the industrial revolution. Only in the present rich, developed countries is there 'malaise, mass neurosis and free floating violence' and, in seeking the cure for ourselves, we may eventually be able to share with the present under-developed states a way of life unencumbered by such disadvantages.

Buckminster Fuller has pointed out that 'the rate at which each successive country, entering industrialisation, accomplishes the full industrialisation . . . constantly accelerates' (*Utopia or Oblivion*, Bantam Books, 1969; Allen Lane, 1970). Russia tooled-up on machinery left on the market because of America's financial crash in 1929. Russia did not buy machines of the type used in England in 1829. She began with a start of one hundred years of other people's development and experience. By the time the technological advance Alvin Toffler calls the 'super-industrial revolution' (*Future Shock*, Bodley Head, 1971) reaches the remote villages of Asia, Africa and South America, perhaps we can have advanced to the stage where the way of life into which they are absorbed is not that of 'malaise, mass neurosis and free floating violence' but one that offers undoubted benefit – civilization at its best.

What sort of future do we want?

All the great civilizations of the past have been slave states. Slaves have performed all the arduous, dull and dangerous work, leaving the free citizens time to study, to travel and to create. Engineers can now give us slave labour again, but this time without degrading any human being.

In the chapters that follow, I shall describe a way of life derived from, and made practical by, machines now existing in plan, in prototype or in projected development. They range from robots to computers to telechiric engineering, and every one of them could be in use before the end of the century, given sufficient public interest and financial backing. These machines could free humans to the point where wage-earners would only have to work a 40,000-hour working life, a maximum twenty-hour week, leaving the rest of their time free to develop all that is highest in mankind.

I have been told that I am over-idealistic in thinking that this is what people would do with free time, and certainly there has been plenty of publicity lately, through films, plays, writing and television, for what the zoologist, Desmond Morris, has called 'the naked ape'. But I believe there is angel in us as well as ape. I think the preoccupation with our more selfish instincts is as mean and limited an image of truth as the selfishness it condones. Love and courage, generosity, tolerance and self-control are no less admirable today than they have ever been, nor are they less often practised: they are simply receiving less recognition and encouragement, and this, in itself, is not good for society. Our recognized 'good' must be a 'good' that benefits us all. The urge to do well, to be approved, is stronger in us than the urge to fail. Our aggressive and go-getting instincts are not bad in themselves. We sometimes need the spur of aggression to bring out the best in us. Equally, though, we need approval for the achievements of our aggression. Public opinion too often gives approval to man's ability to grab more in material wealth than his neighbours.

Is that really what we admire? Would we prefer our leaders to have three cars, half a dozen television sets and their hands out for a quick bribe, as has been known often enough among minor tyrants of the modern world? Or would we rather have men who hold ideals of service to their community and of responsibility to their fellow men? I am sure the latter choice would still be made by most people. The majority of us are still, basically, idealists. All we lack is the strength of purpose and the co-ordination to see our ideals realized. I shall argue that we must strengthen this purpose. We must make our governments enforce our ideals through our laws and the way we spend our public money.

Suicide or survival

Political priorities at the present time are nonsense. However, they are based essentially on democracy so that, if the public knows what it wants, the politicians have to give the public what it wants. If service to mankind became society's demand then I, even as only one inventor seeking new ways to benefit those fellow human beings who seem most in need of help, could complete work now being done in my laboratory to make life easier for the sick and handicapped, to develop telechiric machines to do mining and other dangerous work by remote control, and to make robots that could relieve people from all monotonous, repetitive work in factories.

Machines that could improve the quality of human life

I began designing robots when I was ten. I knew nothing of electronics in those days, of course, so I designed only mechanical robots. I had some idea that they would be triggered into action by sound waves so that I could speak words of command in their 'ears' and they would march away and do my bidding. Needless to say, I never made this work, but it shows that even I, at that time, assumed that a robot would have something of a human nature.

This is not so, of course. Hal, in the film *2001*, was a delightful fictional character but he will never be possible in fact. You cannot build emotions into a machine. The heights and depths of love and hate, comprehended on an intellectual and not merely an instinctive level, are qualities unique to man, and they will remain so. A robot can, of course, be programmed by men to do a great deal of good or a great deal of evil, but it will never have any intrinsic, self-developed moral awareness, however complex its electronic circuits. The housewife's automatic washing machine is a familiar example of a specialized robot: it washes, it rinses, it spins the water out of the clothes and it turns itself off, but it will only fail to do this job if there is a fault in its mechanism, not because it has taken a dislike to human clothing and is running its own campaign for total nudity.

More technically, a robot may be defined as a machine which can be programmed to carry out a series of complex manipulative operations pre-selected from a wide variety of possibilities, including carrying objects from one place to another via a complex path and varying its movements according to its own observations of its surrounding environment.

8

The Americans have already developed two one-handed robots (the Unimate and the Versatran) which can be bought or hired to do the work of one man for twenty-four hours a day without rest or pause. These are, however, senseless robots; that is to say, they can be programmed to a series of several hundred movements which they will repeat identically whether the objects they have to move are there or not and whether they have to knock things out of their way or not.

I, myself, have built a more sophisticated robot with one sight and two touch sensations. This moves along the side of a table until it sees an object on the table, then it stops, puts out a hand, lifts the object off the table and clears it onto a tray. (I will describe this in greater detail in chapter 9.)

The word 'telechirics' has been proposed for all machines in which a human being controls a mechanical hand or hands at a distance, using the natural skill of his own hands and with feedback of sensory information from the region where the artificial hands are working. Remote control hands, seen through closed-circuit television cameras, have already been developed for handling radioactive materials. The same principle could be applied to work in dangerous situations, so that a man could do all such work from a safe comfortable place, and do it just as well as if he were on the spot in, say, a burning building or at the bottom of the sea.

I have in my workshop, already, prototype machines which would enable people paralysed from the waist down to carry on a normal busy life in their own home or in a factory; which would enable the arthritic to walk and exercise without pain; which would carry crippled people up and down stairs. To make these machines available to people who need them takes money all too rarely available in our 'affluent society'. To raise it, I have to persuade a manufacturer that he will make a profit. He will want a market survey and estimates and proof that there are enough sufferers to make it worth his while to tool up for mass production.

Yet if our priorities were the right ones, our first consideration would be for the people who need these machines. Government money would be found to develop such inventions.

A Creative Society

I shall discuss all this in more detail in later chapters where I shall call my ideal society, with its right priorities, the Creative Society. The key to such a way of life would be education in everything that would provide a satisfying answer to the age-old question, 'What is life for?' This education would start by teaching each individual human being to think for him or herself, to be responsible for him or herself and to other people, and to find the greatest possible sense of self-fulfilment and satisfaction through creative activity, whether this was in the arts, in craftwork, in invention, in research, in exploration in any field, or in teamwork on some socially desirable project.

It is hard to define 'creativeness' so as to convey the sense of self-fulfilment I mean in choosing this word as the name for a new society, but I see it as embodying originality, highly trained sensory-motor skills, aesthetic appreciativeness and the striving for high quality that lies in all our natures. A Creative Society would regain for us a sense of high quality in our daily living, the 'zest' felt by the English country people of the eighteenth century.

We would find this zest and quality in our work, in human relationships, in education and in service to others. For this to be most practically achieved, I have suggested that people should live in neighbourhoods or communities: individual, village-sized communities or multiple communities linked to form a city. There would be no set way of life for any one community: it could be as different from its neighbours as historical or cultural patterns, or people's desire for social experiment, would make it. But communities, as a way of life, could supply such basic human needs as the chance for everyone to belong to a group, with all the social protection and stability that can afford, the chance for everyone easily to obtain the basic essentials for comfortable everyday living, the chance for travel or other change in the pattern of an individual's living habits without harmful loneliness or disorientation, and the chance to live in an individually chosen way, regardless of race-origin, national language or even, in most cases, the fact of working for a firm in a different culture or location.

As I have said, I am an optimist. I have envisaged my Creative Society as being established by about the year 2000, when I may even still be alive to see it: but I am a realist, too. I think the chances of our saving ourselves are only, in the present climate of opinion, about one in ten. Only if millions of ordinary people begin to want to find a better way of life and make a conscious effort to compel their governments to give them what they want will our grandchildren have any sort of bearable existence – and I have baby grandchildren. I want them to have a bearable existence. I want them, at the end of their lives, to be able to look back and think 'my life was worth while'. That is the only criterion by which we can judge a social system, that it makes people feel their lives are worth while. Our present social system does not do this. I put forward, here, for consideration, one possible alternative.

2

The Industrial Revolution

The first hundred years

Industrialization might be said to have begun with the man who invented the wheel, some time before 3000 B.C., or with the Chinese genius who revolutionized agriculture by inventing the animal-collar so that horses could be yoked to a plough (an invention which reached Europe in the ninth century A.D.). An anonymous Roman in the second half of the fourth century A.D. put forward plans for ox-powered paddle-boats, pontoon bridges and mobile field-artillery, but his memorandum was pigeon-holed by a civil servant and lost in the filing system for centuries to come. Leonardo da Vinci drew plans for cannons, tanks, submarines, looms, screw-cutting machines, cranes, presses, helicopters, parachutes, hydraulic machines and covered chariots. None of these inventions, however, altered the way of life of a large proportion of the earth's inhabitants. The power revolution which began in England in the middle of the eighteenth century changed the world for all time.

At first this spate of invention was, socially, all gain. Blind Jack Metcalfe linked Yorkshire and Lancashire by building good roads from Stockport to Mottram Langley and Bumby to Skipton. Metcalfe was the forerunner of John Loudon McAdam, who standardized roads, by 1815, to a ten-inch thickness on rural subsoil with a surface of stones mixed with sand and earth and a top dressing of 'small cubical fragments, none weighing more than six ounces' (*A Social History of Engineering*, W. H. G. Armytage, Faber, 1961, from which many of the facts for this and the next chapter have been taken).

As early as 1711, Thomas Newcomen, who was a supplier of iron tools to the Devonshire tin mines, invented the first steam-beam piston-pumping engine, which raised 120 gallons of water a minute over 153 feet near Dudley in Worcestershire. At this time the Newcomen engine had an overall thermal efficiency of 0·5 per cent. The engine, because of its high fuel consumption, greatly stimulated coal production, while production of the engine was stimulated, in turn, by the need to pump water from the mines. In the great coalfields of Tyneside, for example, 137 Newcomen engines were constructed and in use by 1778.

Newcomen died in 1729 and his company's patent on the engine ran out in 1733. After this, improvements were made by a number of people, including John Smeaton, who made the first blast-furnace-blowing machinery for the Carron Ironworks in Scotland and brought the thermal efficiency of the Newcomen engine up to 1·4 per cent by 1774. A Newcomen engine used in the practical physics course at the University of Glasgow broke down in 1763–4 and was mended by James Watt, a twenty-seven-year-old instrument mechanic who saw its salient defects and, by 1769, built a one-cylinder steam-beam engine with a separate condenser and steam jacket and a closed top cylinder.

In 1767 Watt was offered a partnership by a hardware manufacturer, Matthew Boulton, who financed Watt's development of his steam-engine to the point where, by 1785–8, Watt could build a rotative-beam engine fitted with a centrifugal governor acting on the steam throttle valve to regulate the power. This was installed in the Albion Flour Mills at Blackfriars. By 1786 Watt's engines were driving a paper mill, a corn mill and a cotton-spinning mill and supplying power to a brewery and Wilkinson's iron works. Since Watt's engines replaced horses, their power was calculated in terms of horse-power, a fixed unit which Watt introduced: 33,000 foot pounds per minute. It was only the electrical age that named its unit of power in Watt's honour.

The decade that saw the patenting of Watt's steam-engine also saw the patenting of Arkwright's spinning machine. This consisted of 'four pairs of rollers, rotating with progressive rapidity to draw cotton thread out with ever increasing fineness' (W. H. G. Armytage, op. cit.). Arkwright's mass production of thread by the rotatory power of a mill was the climax of thirty-eight years of progressive invention in the textile trade, including Kay's flying shuttle, Hargreaves's spinning jenny, Crompton's improvement in the fineness of yarn and Cartwright and Horrocks's improvements in spinning methods.

None of these machines were wholly satisfactory when made of wood, so the demand for iron increased, a material used by Richard Trevithick in his adaptation of Watt's steam-engine to power steam-boats, road-engines and locomotives. This was after the expiry of

Watt's patent in 1800. 'On Christmas Eve, 1801, Trevithick got his first steam car under way up a steep hill. Though its boiler could not keep up enough steam and though it was inadvertently destroyed through being left unattended with the fire withdrawn, it made history. Steam propulsion had arrived' (W. H. G. Armytage, op. cit.).

Trevithick built a second steam-car which he sent to London and another which he ran on rails in Wales. In 1805 he sent two railway locomotives to Newcastle and in 1806 he sent three steam-dredgers to work on the Thames. He also, in Cornwall, applied a steam-engine to agriculture for threshing, grinding, sowing and ploughing.

Meanwhile, a young plugman at Dewley Colliery near Newcastle was learning, at the age of seventeen, to read and write at night school. His name was George Stephenson.

G. M. Trevelyan writes, of the Industrial Revolution, in *British History in the Nineteenth Century and After* (Longman, 1922):

> the men who made and mended the machines were indeed the bodyguard. They were usually better paid than their fellow-workmen, they often took the lead in educational and political movements. They were less looked down upon by employers, who had to consult them and to bow to their technical knowledge. They were in the forefront of progress and invention and rejoiced in the sense of leading the new age. Such workmen were the Stephensons of Tyneside: there was nothing 'middle class' about the origins of the man who invented the locomotive, after having taught himself to read at the age of seventeen.
>
> It is indeed easier to reconstruct the early history of the coal-miners and textile hands than that of the mechanics and engineers, because the latter were scattered up and down the country. But any picture of the earliest and worst stage of the Industrial Revolution is too black if it omits the life of the mechanics. The motto of the coming age was 'self-help', a doctrine that left behind many of the weaker and less fortunate . . .

Satanic mills

Invention began to bring disadvantages. The social system was disrupted. Village life no longer 'embraced the chief daily concerns of the majority of Englishmen'. Yeomen and labourers no longer carried on 'various branches of manufacture in their own cottages' (G. M. Trevelyan, op. cit.).

Machines could manufacture much more cheaply than a craftsman. Added to this, improvements in agricultural methods led landlords to enclose, between 1760 and 1840, most of the common land on which the cottagers had grazed animals and gathered firewood. With both these sources of income gone, therefore, the poorest of the villagers began to face starvation and to drift to the towns in search of work in the new factories. They found factory life offered them little better conditions.

> Employers, especially in the textile industry, were often
> a new order of men, risen from the ranks by their energy in
> seizing the opportunities of the new industrial situation. A
> workman who had toiled at the hand-loom in his cottage might
> borrow £100 to start as a small employer with the new
> machines . . . The first generation of these men had the defects
> as well as the merits of pioneers. A common type of
> 'millowner' in the days of the younger Pitt was a hard-bitten
> north-country working-man, of no education and great force of
> character, taking little stock of his social or political relations with
> the outer world, allowing neither leisure nor recreation to himself
> or to his hands, but managing somehow to convert the original
> £100 that he had borrowed into a solvent 'mill', the prison
> house of children. (G. M. Trevelyan, op. cit.)

By 1806, cotton was supplying one-third of the total of British exports and a second generation of industrialists, 'real capitalist employers', had

> great assemblies of working-people and an increase in the
> proportion of skilled mechanics . . . The employees, now
> accumulated in one mill by hundreds instead of by scores, could
> not long fail to combine for economic and political action.
> The new type of large millowner had a secure financial position,
> more education and sometimes more enlightenment. Individuals
> of this class introduced factory conditions which inspectors in a
> later time could enforce as standards . . . [so that] if the cotton
> industry showed England the way into some of the worst miseries
> of the Industrial Revolution, it also showed the way out.
> (G. M. Trevelyan, op. cit.)

Women and children, of course, were not only used in the textile industry but also in coal mining. 'Women were used as beasts of burden and children worked in the dark, sometimes for fourteen hours' (G. M. Trevelyan, op. cit.), even as late as 1842 when a Royal Commission on Mines was appointed to look into working conditions.

Canals and railways

Coal was mostly transported by canal before 1830, the British having learnt canal construction from the French before the Napoleonic wars. Notable among the canal builders was the Duke of Bridgewater, who saw the Canal du Midi in 1753, and who employed James Brindley to construct a canal which crossed the River Irwell by aqueduct and halved the price of coal in Manchester. This was the first of about 365 canals built under Brindley's direction and emulated by people like Josiah Wedgwood, who was treasurer of the Mersey–Trent Canal, which brought Cornish china clay to his famous Etruria factory.

The greatest canal builder of all, however, was Thomas Telford, who finished the Caledonian Canal in 1822, after making 920 miles of new road, realigning 28 miles of military road and building over 100 bridges to transform the Highlands of Scotland; meanwhile finding time to build canals between the Baltic and the North Sea (the Gotha Canal) and a suspension bridge over the Menai Straits.

By 1829, however, manufacturers were finding canal transport too slow. Financiers looked for a faster means of moving goods and turned to steam-locomotion which, under George Stephenson, was beginning to prove practicable. Stephenson had become interested in steam through experiments made by William Hedley at Wylam Colliery and, in 1813, Stephenson began to build engines which could draw a load of thirty tons at four miles an hour up an incline of 1:450.

In 1821 he was appointed engineer for the proposed Stockton and Darlington Railway, where he suggested that the rails should be of wrought rather than cast iron. The success of this project encouraged promoters to approach Stephenson with the idea of a railway linking Manchester and Liverpool, which was opened on 15 September 1830, and began the great railway boom which led to some 1,000 miles of track having been laid in the British Isles by the middle of the nineteenth century.

Nineteenth-century pollution

The steam-engines spewed out clouds of black smoke. So did the factory chimneys. For all the increased speed and prosperity of the industrial age, its drawbacks were keeping pace.

Early Victorian towns had to be seen and smelt to be appreciated. The oldest necessities for people living in cities are a constant supply of fresh water, facilities for disposal of excrement and the dissipation of malodorous results of earning a living. All these problems . . . in the hasty expansion of towns, had not been satisfactorily solved. The death rate, which had been falling steadily, suddenly began to rise in 1830. At Birmingham and Bristol it nearly doubled between 1831 and 1841 . . . while in Leeds, Manchester and Liverpool the increase was alarming. (W. H. G. Armytage, op. cit.)

It was three times the present death-rate.

In 1838 Southwood Smith, an admirer of that early sociologist, Jeremy Bentham, conducted an inquiry into the health of twenty London boroughs and unions and published a report which was historic in proving and publicizing for the first time the truth that epidemics of plague and fever were the products of bad sanitation. Statistics of the time showed that bad sanitation alone was responsible for over 40,000 deaths a year.

Southwood Smith helped to form associations to improve the houses of the working class and joined with Edwin Chadwick, secretary of the Poor Law Board, to produce a *Report on the Sanitary Conditions of the Labouring Population of Great Britain* (1842) which said that 'Aid must be sought from the science of the Civil Engineer', an idea Chadwick was given by John Roe, engineer to the Holborn and Finsbury Commission of Sewers. Together they insisted that sanitation should be hydraulic, arterial and water-carried, which meant that a considerable supply of water had to be laid on to every house to flush away the excrement and to carry away sewage in pipe drains (instead of the open channels then in use).

In August 1848 a State Board was set up in Britain which, although it was short-lived, saw the beginning of a twenty-year construction programme, largely carried out by Joseph Bazalgette of the Metropolitan Board of Works, in which 83 miles of sewers were laid, draining 100

17

square miles of the then largest city in the world, London. This was the first really large-scale work on which Portland cement was used, and a technique was patented of coating heated metal pipes with coal oil to resist corrosion. Creosote was also used and, eventually, chlorine in the drinking water, introduced in 1897. All these products encouraged developments in the chemical industry.

Bad sanitation was only one aspect of the environmental deterioration brought about by the Industrial Revolution. Aesthetic standards in manufactured objects declined as well.

> In the midst of this breathless race [for production] no time was left to refine all those innumerable innovations which swamped producer and consumer. With the extinction of the medieval craftsman, the shape and appearance of all products were left to the uneducated manufacturer. Designers of some standing had not penetrated into industry, artists kept aloof and the workman had no say in artistic matters. (N. Pevsner, *Pioneers of Modern Design*, Faber, 1936; Penguin, 1960.)

Concern about this situation, however, was being expressed among the educated upper classes and even at government level, because it was seen that an expanding industrial economy would depend on industry's ability to satisfy the tastes of consumers at home and abroad. Official action was taken in 1836 by the Ewart Committee, which was set up to inquire into 'the best means of extending a knowledge of the arts and of the principles of design among the people, especially the manufacturing population'. This led to the establishment of a National School of Design and to the Victoria and Albert Museum, then called the Museum of Ornamental Art.

Concern was also expressed in publications such as the *Journal of Design and Manufactures*, founded by Henry Cole, and by critical letters to the press expressing horror at some of the products shown in the Great Exhibition of 1851.

This Exhibition, of course, was housed in Joseph Paxton's Crystal Palace – 900,000 feet of glass fastened to a graceful web-like structure of 3,300 columns and 2,300 girders which covered 18 acres of Hyde Park. Paxton had begun his working life as the Duke of Devonshire's head-gardener at Chatsworth. He designed the Crystal Palace in ten days, during which he also kept an engagement to watch a tube of the Menai Bridge being floated into position and attended a meeting of a

3 Small-scale working model of mechanical elephant designed for rough-country load-carrying and a wide range of jobs required in developing virgin land for agricultural purposes. The legs of the 'centipede' track are individually sprung, giving the machine a capability of climbing vertical objects up to one-and-a-half metres high in the proposed full-sized version. The machine could also cross rivers and lakes.

4 An example of a telechiric machine used to handle radioactive substances in the U.K. Atomic Energy Authority establishment at Harwell. Such machines could be developed to allow other difficult or dangerous work (mining, oil prospecting and even surgery) to be carried out by remote control.

railway court at Derby. The Crystal Palace was probably the first prefabricated building and was erected in seventeen weeks. It was a lot more beautiful than many of the manufactured objects displayed in it. As Pevsner (op. cit.) says:

> Sham materials and sham techniques were dominant all through industry. Skilled craftsmanship, still so admirable when Chippendale and Wedgwood were at work, was replaced by mechanical routine. Demand was increasing from year to year, but demand from an uneducated public, a public with either too much money and no time or with no money and no time.

John Ruskin wrote the *Seven Lamps of Architecture* in 1849, in which the first lamp was sacrifice (the dedication of a man's craft to God) and the second lamp was truth. Truth, to Ruskin, was making by hand and with joy, and in this belief he was followed by William Morris, who saw machines as the destroyers of truth and said 'production by machinery is altogether an evil'.

Yet Morris found he could not produce beautiful things by hand-craft methods at a price ordinary people could afford and he died disillusioned, leaving it to his follower, C. R. Ashbee, one of the leaders of the Arts and Crafts Movement, to say, 'Modern civilization rests on machinery, and no system for the encouragement or the endowment of the teaching of the arts can be sound that does not recognize this.'

Steamboats and electricity

Meanwhile, the great reciprocating complex of industrialization, sustained and accelerated by the railway, was still further extended by the steamboat. In this, several railway contractors had a hand, notably Isambard Kingdom Brunel, who had built the Great Western Railway. Brunel insisted that a steamship could sail to New York without refuelling, and proved his point with the *Great Western*, built of oak, and the *Great Britain*, built of iron.

In 1852 Brunel began to build the *Great Eastern*, an iron double-hulled steamship weighing 18,915 tons and designed to sail to the East Indies and Australia. This ship made use of three novelties: (a) an experimental tank by William Froude, designed for model studies on problems of stability and resistance; (b) steam steering gear designed by J. M. Gray, probably the first successful application of the hydraulic

C

servo or follow-up mechanism; (c) the Tangye Brothers' hydraulic presses, which were used for launching.

In 1864 the *Great Eastern* was used in the laying of the first successful transatlantic telegraph cable. The electric telegraph had its origins in the work of Michael Faraday, who produced the first dynamo, but electricity was to owe much of its early practical application to a Salford brewer, James Prescott Joule, who reported the results of his private experiments in William Sturgeon's journal *Annals of Electricity*. Sturgeon had discovered, in 1823, the soft iron electromagnet which was to lead to Faraday's construction of a dynamo. The *Annals of Electricity*, established in 1836, was the first electrical journal to be published in England. 'I can hardly doubt,' Joule wrote in it, 'that electromagnetism will ultimately be substituted for steam to propel machinery.'

In 1843 he announced his discovery of the fact (soon to become the first law of thermodynamics) that the quantity of heat capable of increasing the temperature of a pound of water by one degree Fahrenheit is equal to a mechanical force capable of raising 838 pounds to a height of one foot.

By 1849 Joule had established the indestructibility of energy, the mechanical equivalent of heat and the existence of an absolute zero of temperature.

Perhaps the most important discovery of this mid-nineteenth-century period, however, was Henry Bessemer's almost accidental finding of 'the Bessemer process' to produce cheap steel. At that time, in 1855, during the Crimean War, steel for tools had to be made in small crucibles, and wrought iron was made by strong men stirring semi-liquid metal in tiny furnaces. Steel cost £60 a ton until Bessemer, experimenting with perfecting a patent for giving rotation to an elongated projectile, noticed that a draught of air decarbonized two bars of pig-iron lying on the rim of his furnace. This led to the discovery of his method of forcing air by blower through molten cast iron to oxidize the carbon and produce steel. In December 1855 he patented what was in essence the Bessemer converter.

In August the following year, Bessemer read a paper to the British Association on his process, but the Sheffield Ironmasters would not adopt it, so Bessemer, in partnership with the Galloway Brothers of Manchester and others, set up a foundry in Sheffield from which they were soon able to offer steel at a very low price. This enterprise made a fortune for Bessemer and everyone else concerned with it.

With part of this fortune, Bessemer and others initiated a college of practical engineering at Muswell Hill, near London, which opened in September 1881. This college, under the direction of John Bourne, was virtually the first institution to offer formal training to the engineer. Engineering had become a profession.

3

The Industrial
Revolution

The second hundred years

Once started on its way, the technological juggernaut steadily gained speed. Invention followed upon invention, development upon development, to the point where it has become only practical, here, to remind readers of the larger landmarks in the story of industrial growth. I should like to do this, however, to demonstrate the scale of inventive progression during this period and the role that scientists and engineers played in it. Only if we remember the speed and impact on every aspect of life of this explosive technological growth can we consider (as I shall do in later chapters of this book) its social significance and that of further expansion of the same kind.

I shall therefore briefly outline the stories of: (1) the great chemical discoveries which led to plastics and synthetic fibres; (2) the invention of the internal combustion engine and its use in road and air transport; (3) the development of gas, electricity and oil as sources of power; and (4) explosives and nuclear power.

Chemical technology

One of the earliest chemists was the great alchemist, Jabiribn Hayyan, a notable figure at the court of Haroun-al-Rashid. He combined sulphur and mercury and obtained cinnabar, and also discovered nitric acid.

In the Middle Ages Paracelsus, in Germany, founded a school for chemists who experimented with distillation to find materials to serve the mining industry. Paracelsus was the forerunner of the great nine-teenth-century German chemists, including Friedrich Wöhler, who first discovered metallic aluminium and isolated beryllium (in 1827 and 1828); R. W. von Bunsen, who was first to obtain metallic magnesium by electrolysis, to invent the carbon-zinc electric cell, the burner known by his name and calorimeters for ice and vapour; and Justus von Liebig, whose laboratory at Giessen became a nursery for scientists and whose pupil, A. W. Hofmann, was the first director of the Royal College of Chemistry, opened in London in 1845.

Hofmann's pupils and assistants literally created the synthetic dye-stuffs industry in England. So great was their influence that when Hofmann returned to Germany in 1864 and was followed by some of his assistants, industrialists became alarmed. Luckily, at this time Ivan Levinstein founded a dyestuff works near Manchester and also helped to establish the Society of Chemical Industry in 1881.

Two years after this Society was founded, Sir Joseph Wilson Swan, looking for a satisfactory filament for his electric light bulb, forced nitro-cellulose, dissolved in acetic acid, through a small hole in a coagulating bath of alcohol. He and his assistants then treated the resultant fibres with ammonium sulphide to neutralize the inflammable elements.

This fibre was no good for Swan's intended purpose, but 'with that imaginative insight which characterises the successful applied scientists', says W. H. G. Armytage in *A Social History of Engineering* (Faber, 1961), Swan 'saw that what he had worked on as a potential filament for a light bulb could be a man-made fibre and at the Inventors' Exhibition of 1885 table mats, crocheted from this artificial silk, were exhibited by his wife'.

C. F. Cross and E. J. Bevan, two chemists trained in Manchester, worked on Swan's filament and discovered viscose. Courtaulds purchased the patents and by 1913 Britain was providing 6,000,000 lb. of rayon a year, 27 per cent of the world output. Courtaulds also opened a plant in America and by 1927 were producing half the total world output of rayon.

In 1940 a young co-worker of C. F. Cross, in the laboratory of the Calico Printers' Association at Accrington, discovered another new fibre from ethylene glycol (which motorists know as anti-freeze) and terephthalic acid. The name of the assistant was G. J. Whinfield and his new fibre was called terylene.

The development of another kind of plastics material began when the bicycle and, later, the motor-car led to a search for synthetic rubber. In 1860 Greville Williams isolated isoprene, and in 1879 Bouchardat showed that a rubbery substance could be produced from isoprene by strong hydrochloric acid. In 1884 Sir William Tilden made isoprene

23

from turpentine, and technological development during the First World War, particularly in Germany, led to the production of buna rubbers from coal, limestone and ultimately petroleum. The Second World War provided a need which led to the bonding of this rubber to metal, notably on tank wheels.

Meanwhile, in the 1860s, the British Xylonite Company and the Albany Dental Manufacturing Company had produced substitutes for ivory, tortoiseshell and mother-of-pearl. Science students like H. G. Wells wore celluloid collars. In 1890 A. Spittler, in Germany, accidentally mixed sour milk and formaldehyde, producing casein. In 1909 Dr Baekeland, in America, combined formaldehyde and phenol and produced bakelite.

Again it was the Second World War that saw the real advance in developing this type of plastic material, however. The demand for synthetic rubber, improved techniques for processing petroleum, a large demand for coke which produced quantities of tar, all led to the production of the cyclic aromatics which were then used to make plastics, insecticides, soaps and solvents. A small proportion of benzene so produced was also used for nylon which, in turn, was used for tow ropes and parachutes during the war and, after the war, developed as materials for clothing, household utensils, industrial belting, cordage, gear wheels, bearings, lenses and many other uses (see p. 30).

The internal combustion engine

Though many British proposals were put forward for utilizing volatile fuels before 1836, after this date most pioneer work concerning the internal combustion engine was carried out in France, Germany and America. In America, George Brayton of Boston patented the first engine to use petroleum as fuel in 1872, and in 1877 a German company at Deutz owned by Nicolaus Otto and Eugen Langen, with Gottlieb Daimler as their technical director, patented an eight horse-power gas-engine, which ran at 150 to 180 strokes to the minute. In 1884 Daimler left to set up his own workshop at Canstatt and in 1885 produced a high-speed motor which could drive a wooden cycle along a road.

The invention of the pneumatic rubber tyre by John Boyd Dunlop in 1888 enabled the motor-car to become a practical proposition and, in England, where progress in road transport had been discouraged by restrictive laws passed in 1865 at the prompting of horse and railway interests, parliament rescinded its insistence on a crew of two in motor vehicles and increased the car's permitted speed to 12 mph. After this, Daimler cars began to be manufactured in England, at Coventry, and 'bus companies, like Leylands, were founded soon after the turn of the century. Rolls-Royce was launched as a public company in 1906 and in 1911 the Ford Motor Company began to produce the Model T at Old Trafford.

By 1904 there were over 17,000 motor vehicles on the road in England and the Cycle Engineers Institute added 'Automobile' to their title. The first president of the Automobile and Cycle Engineers Institute, under this new title, was Herbert Austin of the Wolseley Company.

In 1913, to cope with the enormous demands for his car, Henry Ford, in America, set up a moving assembly line which enabled a chassis to be produced in 1 hour 33 minutes, as opposed to 12 hours 28 minutes before that time. In the following year he was producing nearly 300,000 cars a year: traffic jams and production engineering were born in the year that the First World War began.

Incidentally, it is worth noting that Henry Ford drove his car '999' at 91·4 mph, so that motor transport had already reached its top feasible cruising speed on roads as early as 1904. Further developments have merely been 'cosmetic'.

By 1920 there were 650,148 motor vehicles on the roads in Britain and by 1938 British firms were producing about 450,000 motor vehicles annually, second only to the United States, with Germany our near rival. The car was only one force in the social revolution which was following the industrial one, but it was an important factor, equal to the radio (see p. 29) in levelling social classes, in widening people's horizons and bringing them together. The motor-car and coach needed better roads, and better roads, in turn, encouraged motoring. Village isolation was ended and a new type of living community grew up: because people could live farther from the centre of towns and from their work, suburban housing estates began to be built along the roads and over the farmlands of Europe and America.

Other industries, too, were affected by the car. ICI, experimenting with plastics to serve the motor trade, discovered polythene. Food industries, also, were encouraged by the increased demand for picnic foods, chocolate bars and ice-cream. The cosmetics industry grew up as women ceased to be house-bound, but drove out with their families at weekends, stopping to eat strawberries-and-cream teas or to dine out at road-houses.

Not until the 1960s, however, when almost every family in Britain and America owned a car, did it seem to occur to anyone that these delightful mobile private sitting-rooms were emitting carbon-monoxide and other poisons from their exhausts in proportions up to 10 per cent of the exhaust gases and that this, in sufficient quantities, might end by poisoning the air we breathe.

In the meantime, powered flight had been developed, beginning on 17 December 1903, when Wilbur and Orville Wright first became airborne at Kitty Hawk. In 1909 Blériot crossed the channel by plane and in 1910 Hugo Junkers took out a patent for an all-wing airplane, Eustace Short built a factory at Shellbeach, and A. V. Roe developed a biplane of his own design. By 1912, at British Army manœuvres, the Royal Flying Corps could provide two squadrons for reconnaissance, while Germany was running an internal civil aviation service. In 1918 planes were used for bombing in France and patrol work in the Middle East, and by 1924 Imperial Airways was formed to amalgamate nearly all the small British civil airline companies.

However, it is interesting to note that when, in 1912, Lord Fisher asked Charles Parsons if he could build an internal combustion turbine *for ships*, Parsons replied that he did not think it would be possible.

In 1926, the year before Lindberg flew the Atlantic, Dr A. A. Griffiths of the Royal Aeronautical Establishment suggested that a gas turbine engine was a feasible proposition for aircraft, and an air force officer, Frank Whittle, patented one in 1930 with a centrifugal compressor for the turbine as a source of a high-velocity propulsion jet. The Germans took jet-engines more seriously, and by August 1939 had the He 178 in the air – in time, of course, for the beginning of the Second World War.

During the war, the necessities of aircraft manufacture led to ever improving techniques in such areas as the machining of light alloys, powder metallurgy, and the use of duralumin, beryllium, titanium, iridium, fibreglass and plastic adhesives. Aircraft production, in fact, dominated the economies of all belligerents and the need for 100-octane fuel for planes led to revolutionary developments in petroleum.

Since the war, planes have been produced that fly at supersonic speeds, that take off vertically, that spray crops, that rescue people from the sea. A scientist or engineer or businessman who attends international meetings may travel 3,000,000 miles in his lifetime. Yet this is still in a world where there are millions of people who spend all their lives in one Asian, African or Indian village.

The development of gas, electricity and oil as sources of power

(a) Gas

Napoleon's blockade, in 1805, created a shortage of tallow in Britain and increased, among other things, the price of candles. As a result there was a need to develop substitute illuminants, such as coal gas. In France and England the coking of coal for smelting iron became a major industry for armaments and the gas produced from this was easily tapped.

William Murdock produced gas from coal and illuminated his Soho factory in 1798 and Samuel Clegg, Murdock's pupil, joined the Gas, Light & Coke Company when it was founded in 1812. Clegg laid down the techniques of modern gas engineering whereby gas was scrubbed, measured and stored, and his method of reassuring the Royal Society, who sent a deputation to examine his gas containers for safety, was to drive a hole in the side of one container with a pickaxe and light the gas that then came through.

Clegg's successful demonstration of safety led, first, to the gas illumination of London, and then of Boston (1822), New York (1823), Hanover (1825) and Berlin (1826). However, it was not until the 1880s that Carl Auer perfected a gas mantle. This not only gave better illumination, but paved the way for the use of gas for heating and cooking because it was no longer necessary to make and supply gas of a type and at a pressure to provide a luminous flame.

(b) Electricity

Early experiments with electricity have been talked about in chapter 2. The most successful use in the first three-quarters of the nineteenth century was the development of the electric telegraph system, which culminated in the telephone, patented by Alexander Graham Bell in 1876. But not until Charles Parsons designed the first successful turbo-generator in 1884 could the age of electricity really be said to have begun.

27

The turbine principle at once accelerated the production of electric power, and the Americans C. F. Brush, a former telegraph engineer, and George Westinghouse both established companies in England. In 1880 J. W. Swan had carbonized a thread of dissolved cellulose and thereby made electric lighting feasible. T. A. Edison, who joined forces with Swan in 1883, provided the current and designed the first central electric power station in England.

One of the few indigenous English electrical firms, Crompton & Company, was founded at Chelmsford in 1878 and designed and installed lighting equipment in Windsor Castle, Buckingham Palace, the Law Courts and the Imperial Theatre in Vienna. Both Crompton and Edison, however, were to find a rival in an eighteen-year-old, Sebastian de Ferranti, who, working for Siemens, produced the Ferranti alternator in 1882. This, installed under Cannon Street Railway Station, won Ferranti such recognition that he was able to start an independent business and provide the Grosvenor Gallery Electrical Supply Corporation with a generator, transformers, meters, switches and other equipment. Finding that the noise and dirt of the Grosvenor Gallery was inconvenient, however, Ferranti urged that the whole of London north of the Thames should be supplied from a power station to be built at Deptford, which would have access to coal fuel and cooling water. This power station was finished by 1890.

In 1895, in America, the Niagara Falls were tapped for generating purposes; and in 1896 a hydro-electric station was built at Foyers in Scotland for the British Aluminium Company. These were the first hydraulic turbines. Electricity had enabled engineers to extract aluminium cheaply by the use of an electric arc, and electrothermal techniques now enabled artificial graphite and silicon carbide to be made in quantity. Calcium carbide, too, could be made by heating lime and carbon in electric furnaces. From calcium carbide came acetylene for cutting and welding, and cyanamide, a valuable fertilizer and source of ammonia.

The electrical works themselves effected a revolution in factory design, factories near Berlin, designed by Peter Behrens and Walter Gropius, pioneering the glass and concrete structures we think of as typical of twentieth-century architecture.

Electricity also effected a revolution in transport. An electric railway was opened in Richmond, Virginia, in 1887. In 1897 my father was present as a midshipman on one of the naval piston-engined ships at the Spithead review. They were completely outpaced by Parsons's demonstration launch, the *Turbinia*, named after its electric turbine, which achieved a speed of 34½ knots. By 1907 the Cunard Line had installed 70,000 horse-power electric turbine units in the *Lusitania* and the *Mauretania*, and the British Navy also had begun to change to turbine power.

The Institute of Refrigeration was founded in 1900, heralding not only the frozen food industry but also the freezing of such things as blood plasma, which was going to be essential in the two world wars.

In 1901 Marconi first sent a radio message across the Atlantic, and by 1922 the British Broadcasting Company began its daily programmes.

In 1944 the first practical mechanical computer was made by the initiative of Howard Aiken of Harvard University and the International Business Machines Corporation of America (IBM). ASCC, or the Automatic Sequence Controlled Calculator, stored its numbers in wheels with ten positions, each corresponding to one digit. There were 23 digits in each register, consisting of 24 wheels (one for the sign digit), and 72 registers. Operating under instructions conveyed by punched tapes, ASCC's greatest accomplishment was to calculate the mathematical problems concerned with nuclear fission. This took 103 hours to accomplish.

The development of electronic computers began in 1942, again at Harvard and under Howard Aiken, with the construction of an Electronic Numeral Integrator and Computer (ENIAC). In 1946-9 BINAC was constructed (the Binary Automatic Computer) which had two brain valves which checked each other; and in 1948-51 UNIVAC was made (the Universal Automatic Computer) which was built for the American Statistical State Bureau.

One scientist engaged on the ENIAC project was an English physicist, D. R. Hartree, who built the ACE (Automatic Computing Engine) at the National Physical Laboratories at Teddington. The University of Manchester followed this up, under F. C. Williams FRS, and A. W. Turing, Professor Williams being awarded the first Franklin medal in 1958 for this and other work.

The stage was now set for more rapid development under the National Research Development Corporation in England and IBM in America.

Other electric and electronic devices have, of course, included the cinema, which began with the Edison–Dickson kinetoscope, first used commercially at the Nickelodeon, Pittsburgh, in 1905; and television, born from the British cathode-ray tube, the German scanner and techniques worked out by Americans working for the Bell Telephone Corporation and Westinghouse.

(c) Petroleum

The use of oil as a source of power began with the car industry's demand for petroleum. Up to the First World War, however, much of the petroleum produced was almost a waste product. The process of thermal cracking, introduced by William Burton in 1913, improved techniques that were further developed when tetraethyl lead was introduced in 1920 to stop the 'pinking' of aero engines. Now this lead is a major pollutant.

In 1928 W. H. Carothers became director of a new experimental station run by E. I. du Pont de Nemours and Company, and developed a synthetic rubber known as neoprene, made from acetylene, salt and sulphuric acid. He also investigated the synthesis of polymers of high molecular weight by means of esterification and amide formation, which led to the commercial production of nylon fibre.

> During the second world war the Allied armies used fourteen times as much petrol in a day as the entire Allied armies had used in the whole of the first world war. Airplanes needed 100 octane fuel, explosives called for toluene, the loss of the Malayan rubber resources stimulated the production of butadiene, airfields needed asphalt, radio sets needed plastics and resins, whilst the enormous demand for medicines created a sub-industry of petromedicaments. Anaesthetics like cyclopropane, disinfectants, shock drugs like allonal, vaso-constrictor drugs, diuretics for kidney troubles: all flowed from the catalytic cracking plants in great abundance. Indeed, it has been calculated that half a million compounds can be developed from petroleum if uses can be found for them. Synthetics like Paracril for hoses and gaskets, inner tubes, cattle sprays, hormones, alcohol, ketones, esters, all come from tailored and remodelled molecules which chemical engineers can find in petroleum. Even the waxes that were used to pack other products were obtained from petroleum. (W. H. G. Armytage, op. cit.)

Explosives

The use of gunpowder began to be understood in Europe, gaining its knowledge from China, about the middle of the fourteenth century. Gunpowder was used for mining as well as for war, demand increasing until, in the Franco–British war that followed the French Revolution, the French powder factory at Grenelle, for example, made 22,000,000 lb. of gunpowder in eleven months.

In 1832 Braconnot demonstrated how an explosive substance could be created by the action of nitric acid on cotton. Schönbein's discovery of gun cotton in 1845, and Sobero's of nitroglycerine two years later, led to the invention of dynamite by Alfred Nobel, who went on to develop gelignite, initially for civil engineering purposes. Nobel founded a factory, in 1873, at Ardeer on the Ayrshire coast, which not only produced explosives but also made other nitrocellulose products important in the manufacture of paints, lacquers and leather cloth. The factory also made sulphuric acid for fertilizers and batteries, and gave its name to Ardil, a synthetic fibre developed from peanut protein.

Further refinements in the three major explosives nitroglycerine, picric acid and T.N.T. were made in the 1914–18 war, and by 1918 Britain was producing 1,000 tons of high explosive per day.

In 1927 three German engineers, Rudolf Nebel, Klaus Riedel and Wernher von Braun, built a motor that worked on petrol and liquid oxygen and, four years later, using liquid methane and liquid oxygen, dispatched a rocket from a parade ground at Dessau. In 1937 Braun produced a twenty-five-foot rocket which had a thrust of 3,300 lb. and, after further development during the war, made the V2 rockets which were launched against London between September 1944 and March 1945.

Braun's workshop at Peenemünde was captured by the American Army, who transported it bodily to Whitesands in Mexico and set its staff to work to develop the Viking, the Corporal and other rockets for which new propellants like nitric acid and aniline were devised.

A greater development of the Second World War period, however, was the harnessing of a new source of energy, atomic power, and its use in the bombs that were dropped on Japan. The story of nuclear fission began in 1907, when Ernest Rutherford gathered round him a distinguished team of workers at Manchester University to study radioactivity, a phenomenon discovered by H. Becquerel eleven years

31

earlier. Helped by Hans Geiger, Rutherford devised a method of counting the alpha-particles emitted by radium.

By 1911 Rutherford was able to put forward the theory that the atom contained a nucleus bearing a positive charge, around which revolved a number of negatively charged electrons. Extensions to his laboratory (opened by Sebastian de Ferranti, who was by that time President of the Institution of Electrical Engineers) enabled Rutherford to take in further research students, including Niels Bohr, who put forward a more detailed theory of the structure of the atom. This Rutherford–Bohr theory held the field, and by 1919 Rutherford was using alpha-particles from radium to bombard nitrogen nuclei, which ejected high-speed particles. This unlocked a storehouse of potential energy, investigated from then on in every country in the world where physics was taken seriously. I remember, myself, as an undergraduate in 1936, attending Rutherford's lectures which he gave at the Cavendish.

In 1931 F. W. Aston detected the line of the rare isotope 235 of uranium by spectograph. In 1932 H. C. Urey announced his discovery of an isotope of hydrogen known as deuterium and G. Hertz separated it from hydrogen. Knowledge of the structure of the atomic nucleus was then extended by James Chadwick's discovery of neutrons (or uncharged particles) which were found to be valuable missiles for bombarding nuclei, since they were not deflected by electrical forces in the atom. Fission of U^{235} by neutron bombardment was finally produced in 1938, the year that Rutherford died.

By 1939 many scientists were working on the possibility of separating uranium 235, and in June 1941 the Thomson Committee reported to the British Government that an atom bomb could probably be made before the end of the war. In June 1942 British scientists went to the United States to collaborate on this project and their work contributed to the bombs that destroyed Hiroshima and Nagasaki.

The potential value of atomic power, however, is better illustrated by the fact that the complete fission of all the atoms in one pound of U^{235} liberates as much heat energy as by the complete combustion of 2,500,000 lb. of coal.

After the war, an Atomic Energy Research Station was established at Harwell in Berkshire under Sir John Cockroft and a centre of applied knowledge was established at Risley in Lancashire under Sir Christopher Hinton. Calder Hall was built as the first large-scale nuclear power station in the world supplying public electricity; and further stations were built at Bradwell in Essex; Berkeley in Gloucestershire; Hunterston in Ayrshire; Hinkley Point in Somerset; Trawsfynnyd; Dungeness; Oldbury; Sizewell and Wylfe.

In 1952 America tested her first hydrogen bomb. The impact was so terrible that Winston Churchill asked the BBC not to broadcast discussions about it. A British version of the bomb was detonated at Christmas Island in 1957.

As the carrier of the hydrogen bomb, the Americans envisaged a missile. Various missiles were tested and the Atlas Rocket was made available for British manufacture and modification. Powered by a liquid fuel engine and made by Rolls-Royce under licence, it was known as Blue Streak, but it proved too vulnerable to attack and was abandoned in favour of the American-made missile, Skybolt.

Meanwhile, Germany had climbed onto her economic feet again after the war and had begun to overtake in all branches of technology, including nuclear power, computing and the study of outer space. By 1975 she appears to be likely to have greater knowledge in these spheres than any other country in Europe.

So the power race is not only still being run, it is being run at an ever increasing pace: but I will leave it until the next chapter to discuss the desirability, or otherwise, of this fact.

4

The debit and credit balances

My survey, in the last two chapters, of nineteenth- and twentieth-century technological progress has been necessarily limited. I realize that I have failed to talk about such diversely important discoveries as drugs like the sulphonamides and penicillin on the one hand, and inventions such as the hovercraft, lasers and the radio-telescope on the other. As I have said, my aim has been merely to remind the reader of the acceleration of the growth of applications of scientific knowledge so that we can now consider the implications to society of yet further uncontrolled expansion of the same kind.

Has such expansion, for example, been really all progressive? Are we, on balance, better off than our eighteenth-century ancestors? If the disadvantages are increasingly out-weighing the advantages, what must we do about the situation?

As a scientist, an engineer and an inventor, I am obviously finding cause for anxiety or I should not have been impelled to search for the solutions I shall put forward later in this book, or to write about them. So let us look, first, at the facts that are causing my alarm and make them the debit balance in scales to weigh the value of the technological inventiveness we have just reviewed.

The debit balance

If the industrial and technological revolutions had been controlled, in the first place, by an ideal of service to mankind, with restrictions on any invention that was harmful to man or his environment, there would be no 'debit balance'. The dangers have arisen solely because the motive for development has always been, almost from the first, greed for wealth and for power over other people or other nations. The bad consequences of this profit-based engineering are very serious indeed.

34

They include: (1) the threat of destruction of our whole environment by pollution; (2) malnutrition and the failure to help people in countries not industrially developed; (3) the threat of total annihilation by war-weapons; (4) the exhaustion of the world's natural resources to supply needs created by a policy of advertising and artificial obsolescence; (5) the destruction of the quality of life by noise, dirt, ugliness, monotonous jobs, anti-social housing and the beat-your-neighbour pressures of a one-up-on-the-Jones's objective for society, leading to neuroses, ill-health, loneliness, purposelessness and therefore drug-taking, drunkenness and violence.

(1) The destruction of our environment by pollution

Beside radioactive dusts, the following pollutants are known to be emitted into the atmosphere in substantial quantities as an unintentional result of man's technological activities:

(a) Products of complete combustion (not harmful): CO_2, H_2O.
(b) Products of incomplete combustion or thermal decomposition of hydrocarbons, fats and glycerol: CO, C_nH_m, benzpyrene, aldehydes, partially oxidized hydrocarbons.
(c) Sulphur compounds: SO_2, SO_3, H_2SO_4, H_2S.
(d) Oxides of nitrogen NO_x, especially NO and NO_2.
(e) Chlorine and fluorine compounds, especially HCl and HF.
(f) Arsines.
(g) Hydro cyanide.
(h) Phosgenes.
(i) Ammonia.

Also particles and aerosols such as iron oxide; cement and lime dust; pesticides; Pb compounds; metallic compounds; asbestos; soot and fly ash.

> Sulphur oxides [writes John McHale in *The Ecological Context*, Studio Vista, 1971] . . . harmful aerial pollutant in highly industrialized countries, is expected to show a 75 per cent increase over present levels by 1980. A single fossil fuel power-generating plant may emit several hundred tons of sulphur dioxide per day and, under certain weather conditions, locally overburden the air of a whole city. When this effect is increased by larger

D

multiple fuel uses in dense urban concentrations, the results may be lethally apparent – four thousand persons died, directly or indirectly, from one week of such intense pollution in London in 1952, and one thousand in 1956. It is estimated that each year the United States has 142 million tons of smoke and noxious fumes pumped into its atmosphere – more than 1400 pounds per person. In addition to aerial pollution, it has been calculated that certain elements, for example argon, neon, krypton and so forth, essential to the life maintenance, are now being 'mined' out of the atmosphere by industrial operations at a faster rate than they are being produced by natural processes . . .

Water, a key resource in daily life, agriculture and industry is also in critical balance in many world regions. Approximately 95% of fresh waters are at present used at a greater rate than their precipitation replacement in ground surface waters . . .

Waste disposal, even in the most advanced countries, is still archaic. Those methods used in our larger urban concentrations are little improved from the traditional systems evolved for much smaller and less waste-productive communities of the pre-industrial period. The average city of a half-million people now disposes of 50 million gallons of sewage daily and produces solid wastes of about eight pounds per person each day . . .

Large amounts of soil additives in the form of fertilizers and chemical nutrients are washed off the lands through rainfall, irrigation and drainage into the natural water courses where they disturb the aquatic life balances. The undue growth of algae and plant growths decreases the oxygen supply for fish and other organisms, thus attenuating the self-renewal of the water-system. Again, such problems are not localized. In the case of pesticide 'runoff' from the land and other toxic discharges from domestic and factory sources and so forth, these may be relatively isolated and 'unobjectionable' where they enter upper reaches of streams and rivers. Their concentrated build-up effects may only be felt thousands of miles away – where rivers enter lakes or reach the ocean, for example, as in the massive fish kills, of around 12 million, in the Mississippi and Gulf of Mexico in recent years.

All this, I think, gives some idea of the seriousness of the pollution problem.

(2)   Hunger and the failure to help the people of the under-developed countries

Between 1900 and, say, 1965, the proportion of people in the developed countries attaining economic and physical success to a standard of living and health superior to that ever enjoyed by mankind before this century has risen from 1 per cent to 40 per cent. But in the same period the gap between the standard of living of the well-off 40 per cent, who are mostly in the industrially developed countries, and the remaining 60 per cent has widened. In the under-developed countries, malnutrition is common. At least a third to a half of the world's people suffer from hunger or nutritional deprivation. The average person in the industrial countries eats about 4 lb. of food a day, compared with an average of $1\frac{1}{4}$ lb. in the under-developed countries. Infant deaths per 1,000 in the developing countries are four times as high as in the industrially developed countries, and a man can only expect to live about half as long.

Malnutrition in the early years not only stunts physical growth but also retards mental growth: this leads to the people with problems lacking the will and skill to cope with them. Also, many of the developing countries in which great numbers are undernourished are forced to export food to pay for manufactured goods and materials they cannot produce. One of the key critical factors, here, then, is the parasitic relation of the more advanced countries upon the poorer regions and their failure to take any effective steps to improve this situation.

(3)   Radioactivity and war-machine escalation

The hydrogen bomb exists. Dropped on the ground, it can kill everyone within a ten-mile radius and cause large-scale damage over a fifty-mile radius. Its effects on the atmosphere (no less when such a bomb is exploded in a scientific experiment than when it is exploded in war) distributes poison which can shorten the lives of many hundreds of people and damage millions.

Ritchie Calder, in a presidential address to the Conservation Society in 1968, stated that every young person who grew up any-where in the world during the bomb-testing period has a detectable amount of radio strontium replacing some of the calcium in their bones. This, of course, is far below the medically significant level, but an accumulation could undoubtedly have harmful psychological and genetic effects.

It is certain that if the stockpiles of nuclear weapons now existing were released in war, the result would be the complete destruction of intelligent human life all over the world within a few years.

Even if such weapons are not used in war, they are wasting money and the following chart, reproduced from *The Ecological Context* (op. cit.), demonstrates this simply and explicitly.

Alternative social costs

Negative	v.	Positive
4 attack submarines at $45,000,000 each . . .	would pay for	1 year of agricultural aid for $178,699,760
One $105,000,000 atomic submarine minus missiles	would pay for	$132,095,000 in famine relief aid including freight costs
One $122,600,000 atomic submarine including missiles	would pay for	$150,000,000 in technical aid
One $275,000,000 aircraft carrier	would pay for	$251,000,000 for 12,000 high school dwellings
One $104,616,800 naval weapons plant	would pay for	35 school buildings at $4,000,000 each
One $104,616,800 naval weapons plant	would pay for	26 160-bed hospitals at $4,000,000 each
One $250,000,000 intercontinental ballistic missile base	would pay for	One 1,743,000 kWh capacity hydro-electric dam
14 standard jet bombers at a cost of $8,000,000	would pay for	A school lunch programme of $110,000,000 and serving 14 million children

Negative	*v.*	Positive
One new prototype bomber, fully equipped	would pay for	250,000 teacher salaries this year or 30 science faculties each with 1,000 students or 75 fully-equipped 100-bed hospitals or 50,000 tractors

(4) The exhaustion of the world's natural resources

Man removes from the earth 2,000 million tons of petroleum a year, all of which has taken 250 million years to produce; we use 600 million tons of iron a year, which has taken 2,000 million years to concentrate; we use 4 million tons of lead, which has taken 4,000 million years to concentrate. Petrol and coal are used and gone for ever. Metals can largely be recycled. Even so, the earth's resources can be exhausted within a foreseeable time.

(5) The destruction of the quality of life, or psychological pollution

Neuroses waste time and energy. Whether they take a mild form and only appear as a headache, backache, stomachache, dizziness or pains in the joints, or whether they compel us to walk on the lines of paving stones, go back six times to see if a tap is turned off, or to wash our hands every few minutes, they are taking energy from our lives that could be better spent.

Alivin Toffler wrote in *Future Shock* (Bodley Head, 1970): 'We may define future shock as the distress, both physical and psychological, that arises from an overload of the human organism's physical adaptive systems and its decision-making processes.'

Neuro-psychiatric research has proved that not only illness but death may be linked to the severity of adaptational demands placed on the body. Scientists at the Institute of Community Studies, in London, after studying 4,486 widowers, stated that 'the excess mortality in the first six months (shows that widowerhood) appears to bring in its wake a sudden increment in mortality-rates of something like 40%'.

The death of a spouse is regarded by doctors and psychologists as the single most impactful change in any person's life, but the statistics concerning this emotional shock serve to illustrate the fact that change, anxiety and nervous stress can kill or maim human beings. Emotional exhaustion in the face of mental over-stimulation has led to soldiers in battle becoming apathetic, dull, listless, confused and almost mindless.

In a static society, change is stimulating to everyone. Even in a changing society, a few people thrive on change and deliberately choose it as their way of life. Many more, however, become depressed and disorientated, especially if the social changes happen too quickly. It is now becoming obvious that it is essential for us to control our rate of social change to a pace that gives most people time to understand what is happening, to adapt their own lives and to find a satisfactory role under the new conditions. If we can make new social conditions such that, within them, human beings feel valuable and secure, then there will cease to be difficulties about adaptation. People will move naturally and cheerfully towards such a society, especially if it makes allowance for the infinite variation of individual character.

Conclusions from the 'debit' facts

It is absolutely clear that society cannot go on depriving, threatening, polluting, wasting or changing its values in a haphazard way without reaching a destruction point some time within the next thirty years.

> The nature of the crisis is such that no *local* measures can now, by themselves, be wholly effective or sufficient unless they are considered within the whole system. No piecemeal acts of emergency-pressured political legislation can, alone, do more than postpone catastrophe – perhaps, hopefully, beyond the next election! The socio-political understanding of the larger ecological implications of local actions and decision-making must now be set within a more radically framed series of questions on how they affect, and are affected by, other dimensions of the crisis. Their consideration goes, inexorably, from local to regional to national to international and trans-national consequences and implications. (John McHale, op. cit.)

R. Buckminster Fuller has written in the collection of his lectures that form the book, *Utopia or Oblivion* (Bantam Books, 1969; Allen Lane, 1970):

> success for all humanity can never be accomplished by politics, which is inherently divisive and biased and, to be effective, must eventually have recourse to its ultimate tools of war-making . . . fundamental world peace probably can be accomplished only by a design-science revolution which can and may realise the feasible potential by up-grading the performance per units of resources to provide 100 per cent of humanity with an ever-higher standard of living.

By 'standard of living' is meant *quality of living*, that is to say, not only a high standard of comfort in material terms but also satisfaction in social and emotional terms.

The credit balance

But what do we, as a world community, have to work with? What is the credit balance of technological progress, the other half of our pair of scales? Our greatest gain is surely longevity.

(1) Longevity

Perhaps all man's greatest achievements in the last two hundred years have been in the medical field. Because of these advances we can, in the industrial countries, generally look forward to a life-span double that of our grandfathers. The greatest strides have been made in preventive medicine, health regulation and surgery. We can expect a healthy life long enough to study, to raise children, to use our knowledge to serve our community and even, if we want to, to sit back for a well-earned rest.

(2) Improved agricultural methods

Enough food could be produced to feed the whole world. Towards the end of the nineteenth century, for example, one farmer in the developed countries could provide food for five other people. By 1930, he could produce enough food for ten people; in 1960, twenty-six people; in 1970, forty-five people; all this with the help, not only of mechanization, but also of chemical fertilizers. This has, however, been achieved at great cost in such long-term benefits as the quality of the soil, the depth of its humus, soil erosion through the cutting down of trees and hedges, damage to wild life by insecticides, and noticeable taste and quality deterioration in the food produced.

Therefore the only long-term and realistic solution to the problem of providing good-quality food, for generations to come and for everyone in the world, is to reconceptualize and redesign the whole food production system on a world basis, and through a more integrated and ecologically orientated approach, with regard not only to agriculture but industry, food processing, food distribution and so forth. Ocean farming would have to be developed and artificial protein and natural protein production increased (see chapter 7).

(3) Energy resources

At the present time the world as a whole spends as much on energy as it does on food. This energy goes into four main uses: (a) power for transport; (b) power for home, industry and agriculture; (c) industrial heating, such as metal melting; (d) heating buildings.

This year 17,000 kwh, or about two tons of coal equivalent, will have been consumed for every individual person in the world (about 3,700 million). In the United States, each person uses six times the world average, but this figure is rising by only 1 per cent every year, whereas the world usage per head rises by 3·8 per cent, which means that the world usage is likely to be doubled within the next twenty years.

Assuming that the world population has almost doubled by the year 2000, to around the 7,000 million mark, the world fuel consumption will be almost six times as high as it is at present – $380 \cdot 10^{12}$ kWh or 40,000 million tons of coal equivalent.

Where will this power come from and how can it be used to the greatest advantage?

(a) *Coal* At the moment the world's largest resource of fossil fuels is coal, which results from the deposition of thick layers of woody plant material being squeezed down into layers of hard coal, usually of the order of two metres in thickness, although in Queensland there is a face of coal 150 m thick. Seams half a metre thick are worth working, if the coal is of high quality, and in Britain we have enough proved reserves of coal for 250 years, if we mine it at 200 million tons a year (which has been our approximate rate during the first half of the twentieth century). The United States, Russia and China have sufficient reserves for 1,000 years at their present rate of usage.

With coal, therefore, there is no immediate shortage and the chief problems are those concerned with getting the solid material from the ground to the factory or power station. New solutions will be discussed in chapter 8.

(b) *Liquid and gaseous fuels* Resources of liquid fuel are only about one hundredth those of coal, but the proved reserves are still about fifty times the world's present annual consumption. Liquid and gaseous fuels can only be found where plant matter has decayed underneath a cap or dome of impervious rock, the products being trapped over water in porous rock so that they cannot escape upwards. This means that even when all the possible sites have been explored, including those under the ocean, the total quantity is still likely to be much less than coal. Thus, it could well be that if our usage of liquid fuels continues at its present rate, the world might have, at best, enough for 150 years. However if, as has been happening, world consumption doubles every ten years, then we could well run short early in the next century.

The tar sands of Athabasca in Alberta contain enough oil to provide the world's present usage for fifty years, but it would have to be extracted from the sand by steam washing or distillation, and these methods are much more expensive than just drilling a hole in the ground and pumping out the liquid. Similarly, there is enough oil to supply the world for 150 years in the Colorado oil shales, but here the only way of winning it, as far as can be seen at present, is to excavate or mine the rock and put it through a heating furnace like an old-fashioned gas retort.

Natural gas is in even shorter supply than oil and occurs in similar situations. Also, it may contain a high H_2S content (15 per cent, for example, in French deposits near the Pyrenees). However, unlike oil and coal, it is not impossibly expensive to remove the sulphur from natural gas and part of the cost can be covered by the sale of the sulphur when it has been extracted.

(c) *Nuclear fission* Nuclear fission has been hailed ever since the Second World War as the fuel of the future. It depends on the production of heat by the controlled chain reaction in which a heavy nucleus, bombarded by a neutron which enters it, splits into two roughly equal parts, plus more than one neutron, which is then available to split the next nucleus. Unfortunately, the only element available in nature which can readily undergo fission when entered by slow neutrons is the rare isotope of Uranium 'U^{235}', which occurs to the extent of one part in 150 in natural uranium.

Thus, although 1 kg of U^{235} is equivalent to 4,000 tons of coal, there is not unlimited energy available unless very low-grade ores are used, and these are expensive to concentrate. Moreover, it is necessary to increase the proportion of U^{235} in natural uranium if one wants a compact, high-power output reactor, and this, again, is expensive because no chemical methods can be used because the two isotopes are chemically indistinguishable. Much work is being done on this separation, which has to be based on small physical differences, usually of density. The ultra centrifuge is the latest development.

The breeder reactor uses a blanket of natural uranium or thorium outside a fast reactor and it is possible for one slow neutron to escape into this blanket material and convert it into a new fissionable substance (either plutonium or U^{233}) which is then chemically different from the blanket and can be separated from it. Here again, however, there is a limitation in that the turn-round time (between the first U^{235} being consumed and the replacement fissile element being available) is more than ten years so that, if the world's usage of nuclear energy doubles every ten years, we shall still need a steadily increasing supply of natural uranium and may well exhaust the richer sources of uranium.

Other serious problems with nuclear energy are the danger to human life if there is a breakout of radioactive materials, by accident or sabotage; the disposal of used materials and shut-down reactors; and the vast need for cooling water which can over-heat whole lakes or rivers.

(4) Materials resources

Most analyses of world resource materials deal in 'years of supply in exploitable reserves'. For example:

Aluminium	570 years
Iron	250 years
Zinc	23 years
Copper	29 years
Lead	19 years
Tin	35 years

This, however, fails to take into account the fact that metals are highly recoverable through their scrapping cycles and can therefore be used over and over again. Given abundant supplies of energy through more efficiently controlled use of capital energy sources, man could secure almost inexhaustible supplies of further minerals from the earth's crust, and the potential of the ocean for metals and materials has hardly been touched.

Conclusions

The debit balance is definitely beginning to outweigh the credit balance. We urgently need to reanalyse our industrial systems in terms no longer based on the present production/consumption attitude. The concept of 'spaceship earth' has been used by many people, but it is well summed up by K. E. Boulding in *Environmental Quality in the Growing Economy* (Johns Hopkins Press, for Resources for the Future Inc. 1966):

> The closed economy . . . in which the earth has become a single spaceship, without unlimited reservoirs of anything, either for extraction or for pollution, and in which, therefore, man must find his place in a cyclical ecological system which is capable of continuous reproduction of material form even though it cannot escape having inputs of energy . . .

'Tie in a living tether', G. K. Chesterton wrote in *A Hymn*:

> The prince and priest and thrall
> Bind all our lives together
> Smite us or save us all.

We are all on spaceship earth. Chesterton's hope has come true. And while, to some of us, his class-consciousness seems archaic and slightly ridiculous, it is only fifty years since he wrote these words and there are still some shop-stewards who seem to think in terms of labour/management, 'them' and 'us', let alone viewing world problems in terms of immediate personal responsibility.

Such a man, however, may well be bewildered by a son's university education and success as a 'boss' in industry; and his son's son is probably hitch-hiking through Asia in his college vacation, part of an already international generation, most of whom are eagerly searching for a realistic course in which to steer their 'spaceship'.

I offer my own ideas for a navigational chart in the next few chapters.

5

The Creative Society

Any vision of a future state, whether it is Utopian or the reverse, like George Orwell's *1984*, will necessarily have a cohesion and simplification unlikely to be achieved in any final reality. Also, because I am an engineer and an inventor of machines, the emphasis of my particular Utopia will be upon the possibilities made practicable by hardware which, in turn, will be designed to solve such problems as anti-pollution, conservation of raw materials, frustration, drudgery, and the other social needs I have talked about in chapters 1 and 4.

Since a grab-all society can only lead to man's destruction, I shall now argue for an idealistic society with new ambitions; and since the rejection of material wealth as an ambition means finding an alternative aim that better satisfies man's onward-upward urge, I shall suggest 'creation' as a way of life that could encourage the enlargement of both the individual and the racial mind and spirit.

By 'creation', I mean, as I have said, the encouragement of the inventor–craftsman–artist in mankind; and this, in turn, would of course encourage social experiment. Therefore individual homes, communities and the total world society are all likely to become more and more socially fluid and organic, changing (but at a carefully controlled rate) habits and rules to suit minds that, with ever extended education (in terms of understanding and experience over a wide field), will become, perhaps, in a generation or two, as far removed in outlook and desires from our minds today as, say, the mind of our greatest mathematician or philosopher is far removed from the mind of a stone-age hunter.

Technologically, as we have seen, the world has changed at a very great pace. From the beginning of time until the 1830s, man had never exceeded the speed of a chariot (about 20 mph). A hundred years later he was flying at about 300 mph. Thirty years later still, men in space capsules were circling the earth at 18,000 mph. Until the middle of the fifteenth century, Europe was unlikely to have produced more than 1,000 hand-written books a year. In 1950, Europe produced 120,000 books (new titles, not individual copies) meaning, in terms of building up a library, that what might once have taken a century to get together could now be collected within ten months. Ten years later, however, by the mid-sixties, the output of books had risen to 1,000 titles *per day*. The diversity of knowledge, the rate of learning, is expanding that fast. So is the number of people educated to produce knowledge. As has frequently been pointed out, 90 per cent of all the scientists who have ever lived are alive and working today.

So man, himself, must inevitably change. His brain must evolve. It has a far greater capacity than he uses now. But it seems likely that he will still have much the same physical and emotional needs. Biologically, he cannot change quickly – so the society I shall outline will attempt to serve this comparatively changeless man. A man, we have come to the conclusion in chapter 4, who must live in what is to all practical purposes, if not nominally, a one-world state. Such a world state could only function successfully, however, if it had quick, cheap, foolproof communications systems, so I shall devote the next chapter, chapter 6, to 'World transport in a Creative Society'. Such a world state could also only finally work if there are no 'have nots', no starving people, no one homeless and left out; so I shall write in chapter 7 about possible means of increasing and transporting world food supplies. In chapter 1 I have already talked about freeing mankind from the degradation of having to do monotonous, physically exhausting or unnecessarily dangerous work, and I will describe machines that could take man's place in carrying out such tasks in chapter 8. In chapter 9 I will try to conjure up some sort of picture of what it might be like to live in a home in my Creative Society, although it would be there, in any individual home, that the greatest diversity would be found in a way of life that would have as its whole object the encouragement of people to think for themselves, and to be themselves, and to create with their hands.

Architects' and science fiction writers' visions of future cities have often taken the form of some sort of human ant-heap of megalopolis proportions with blocks of identical fully-automated flats piling up and up to serve a population so enormously increased that only a small

48

proportion of them could find footroom on the earth's surface at any one time.

This seems to me unlikely to become necessary. When a country reaches a certain stage of prosperity and education, especially education for women, the population tends to decline. The population growth rate is already declining in North America, Europe and Russia – in America to only 1·9 children per family, which is less than replacement level. Certainly, for the rest of this century at least, the improvement in medical care, and thus in longevity, will mean that the world population will go on increasing, but with luck it might level out at the present 3½ billion people. At the moment, if the world's surface could be equally divided among us, we should have about ten acres of land apiece – and even at half this acreage we shall hardly be treading on each other's toes, especially as a much greater proportion of the land available could, by that time, be made fertile and habitable (see chapter 7).

One of the least desirable facts of life today is that many people, if they are to find work that pays them well, must live out their lives either in the centre of a big city or in dormitory suburbs where their families feel lonely and cut-off, and to which the wage-earner must drive nose-to-tail with other car drivers in a rush-hour, blocking the roads and filling the city with traffic fumes.

In chapter 1 I talked about the stable, ordered and comparatively happy and prosperous way of life enjoyed by most people at the height, and end, of the agricultural society. At this time, the majority of people lived in villages where they were known and cared about and had their part to play in the community life. Although, in a world society with easy travelling facilities, individuals in any one community would come and go at a far quicker rate than the inhabitants of an eighteenth-century village, I believe that, once people accepted the principle of community living as a way of life, the same sense of security and order and belonging could be achieved again.

Some of these village or city communities would be the villages or cities we know today, of course, but where new communities were built, computer technology might help the planners to create the sort of environments people really needed, rather than sterile 'little boxes on the hillside'.

Architects' work on these lines is probably best summed up by quoting a treatise by Christopher Alexander which won one of the 1965

49

Kaufmann International Design Awards, 'The City is not a Tree'. This was printed in *Design* magazine (February 1965):

> The tree of my title is not a green tree with leaves. It is the name of an abstract structure. I shall contrast it with another, more complex abstract structure called a semi-lattice. The city is a semi-lattice, but it is not a tree. In order to relate these abstract structures to the nature of the city, I must first make a simple distinction.
>
> I want to call those cities which have arisen more or less spontaneously over many, many years 'natural cities'. And I shall call those cities and parts of cities which have been deliberately created by designers and planners 'artificial cities'. Siena, Liverpool, Kyoto, Manhattan are examples of natural cities. Livittown, Chandigarh, and the British New Towns are examples of artificial cities.
>
> It is more and more widely recognised today that there is some essential ingredient missing from artificial cities. When compared with ancient cities that have acquired the patina of life, our modern attempts to create cities artificially are, from a human point of view, entirely unsuccessful.
>
> Architects themselves admit more and more freely that they really like living in old buildings more than new ones. The non-art-loving public at large, instead of being grateful to architects for what they do, regards the onset of modern buildings and modern cities everywhere as an inevitable, rather sad piece of the larger fact that the world is going to the dogs.
>
> It is much too easy to say that these opinions represent only people's unwillingness to forget the past, and their determination to be traditional. For myself, I trust this conservatism. People are usually willing to move with the times. Their growing reluctance to accept the modern city evidently expresses a longing for some real thing, something which for the moment escapes our grasp.
>
> The prospect that we may be turning the world into a place peopled only by little glass and concrete boxes has alarmed many architects, too. To combat the glass box future, many valiant protests and designs have been put forward, all hoping to recreate in modern form the various characteristics of the

natural city which seem to give it life. But so far these designs have only remade the old. They have not been able to create the new.

Outrage, the *Architectural Review*'s campaign against the way in which new construction and telegraph poles are wrecking the English town, based its remedies, essentially, on the idea that the spatial sequence of buildings and open spaces must be controlled if scale is to be preserved – an idea that really derives from Camillo Sitte's book about ancient squares and piazzas . . .

The problem these designers have tried to face is real. It is vital that we discover the property of old towns which gave them life, and get it back into our own artificial cities. But we cannot do this merely by remaking English villages, Italian piazzas and Grand Central Stations. Too many designers today seem to be yearning for the physical and plastic characteristics of the past, instead of searching for the abstract ordering principle which the towns of the past happened to have, and which our modern conceptions of the city have not yet found. These designers fail to put new life into the city, because they merely imitate the appearance of the old, its concrete substance: they fail to unearth its inner nature.

What is the inner nature, the ordering principle, which distinguishes the artificial city from the natural city? You will have guessed from the first paragraph what I believe this ordering principle to be. I believe that a natural city has the organisation of a semi-lattice; but that when we organise a city artificially, we organise it as a tree . . .

The work of trying to understand just what overlap the modern city requires, and trying to put this required overlap into physical and plastic terms, is still going on.

So I shall leave the architectural details to the experts and their computers. The architecture of any community or city would, in any case, vary from place to place, but the principle of community living I believe to be absolutely basic to a world state since it would demand participation from the individual to the greater or less extent to which he would personally wish to become involved; and it would give him great securities in the form of actual physical protection, help in times of stress and freedom from loneliness. If 'human relationships' in the form of basic psychology and sociology, as well as the history and customs of people in various parts of the world, were taught in schools, this might combat the undoubted trend in our present society for more and more people either to drop out or to feel left out.

I shall therefore write about my Creative Society as a world-wide network of communities, ranging in size from the small centre serving a farm area to the up-to-a-dozen or more linked communities that would form a city complex. People would both live in these communities and work in them, freely accessible to each other by video-telephone.

The video-phone has already been produced experimentally, but it requires at least 300 times as much information to be transmitted per second as a normal audio-telephone. Thus it is necessary either to replace the conventional telephone wires with coaxial cables, or with optical fibres which might be developed to convey information superimposed on light beams with a wave length some 10,000 times shorter than short-wave radio, so that each beam could carry 10,000 times as much information. Alternatively, direct laser beams of light might be passed from towers similar to short-wave radio beacons, provided that the means could be found to overcome attenuation in fog.

By the year 2000, it should also be possible for people to carry telephones about with them and to telephone anyone anywhere in the world. This could be done by using a combination of pulse code modulation, optical fibre and radio transmission. Thirty-four binary digits could provide 10^{10} separate telephone numbers, enough for every person in the world to have his own telephone. To save having to press a key thirty-four times, however, the user would carry a magnetic tape record of the numbers belonging to those people he would normally want to call, and could then place this tape on his phone to call a number automatically.

This type of telephoning could be paid for, like most hiring of public services and ordinary shopping, by a credit-card system. The trend towards credit-card payment, together with the allied development of renting instead of buying non-consumable products, is already obvious in the industrial countries. This trend seems to me one which might lead to a way of life particularly suitable to a world community. To be able to hire a car, a house or any other necessary commodity on arrival at any community in the world on presentation of a credit card would solve a lot of the difficulties of freely available across-the-world-in-a-day travel. Credit cards could be automatically checked against their owner's photograph, signature and voice-print by link to a central computer at his bank which would also check whether he had money in his account. For simplicity, it would be an advantage if a world-wide currency system could be established, although it would not be impossible for each national to be debited in his own currency. This credit-card system would avoid all bad debts: without a solvent bank account no one could make a purchase or hire a public service.

The video-phone might also revolutionize businesses. Instead of a large company having its own office in the centre of a city, it could have smaller offices in each city community, or even small offices all over the country, with video-phone links with each other and the rest of the world. The company could also have a central microfilm filing system and computerized information store. There would be no correspondence by letter in the form of typed paper sent through a postal system. Instead, written matter, figures, drawings or any other form of visual information would be transmitted on a video-screen, photographed in the recipient's office, answered in the same way, and then sent with a copy of the answer to the central filing system.

What sort of paid work would still be essential?

Office and factory work would still be necessary. Although, as I have said, machines could be designed to do all the drudgery and dangerous work in the world, human technical skill and intelligence would still be necessary for maintenance, organization, creativity and any job where human emotion, such as sympathy or enthusiasm, was an essential ingredient of the work. This last would include teaching, caring for the sick and elderly, and every aspect of public relations, from diplomacy to salesmanship.

Experience would have to show, however, how much of the work still needed by society would have to be done at set hours and in exchange for money and how much could be done on a voluntary basis in exchange for honour within the community. If world wealth produced by machines could provide every family with a world citizen's right to a good basic standard of living, not everyone might feel it essential to do paid work to earn extra money over and above this basic provision. The need in any society is for each individual member of it to feel that his or her particular qualities are used and appreciated. This need not necessarily be achieved by work in exchange for money. It would depend what the world needed. Social approval for activities would probably grow up naturally from social needs. The best method of apportioning the world's work might be found to be one in which every adult, or every family breadwinner, worked for a twenty-hour or three-day week on a day-time shift system. Or it might be better for the particularly skilled or eager or energetic to work a longer week for, say, a six-hour period each day for only twenty years.

The rule might vary from place to place or time to time, but once the social attitude was established that service and not selfishness was the recognized 'good', individuals would inevitably be affected by community opinion and therefore more likely to conform to social codes of behaviour, especially if these were the tolerant codes of an educated and prosperous society.

Mankind would certainly still need innovators, whether these were inventor–engineers, scientists, mathematicians, philosophers, artists or people who thought up new leisure activities or new directions in which mankind might find a fuller and more enjoyable life. Such people would always form an *avant-garde* and be given special rewards in any society, but whether, in a Creative Society, their reward would take the form of kudos or money or freedom to live a more individualistic life than most members of the world's communities would only evolve from the society's, and these people's, needs.

A secondary range of incentives would have to be offered to all technicians skilled in diagnosing faults, whether these occurred in human beings (doctors or dentists) or in the complex machines, including computers, on which the Creative Society would be so largely dependent. These top technicians could also include detectors of faults in world political organizations (diplomats), commercial organizations (trouble-shooters), and keepers of law and order (judges, lawyers and international crime prevention experts). In the rare case where a fault proved to be a new one, never spotted before (this would apply particularly in things like surgery), the technician would then merit a reward on equal standing with an innovator.

The third category of paid workers who would need to be offered particular incentives would be the organizers, the programmers, and the maintenance technicians. These would range from nurses, through office workers and local police forces to such occupations as machine mechanic.

In all these categories, but particularly in the third one, perhaps special awards could be made for conscientiousness and persistence in overcoming obstacles, virtues all too seldom recognized and rewarded in our present society.

All three categories would include teachers. Education would be a lifelong process. With leisure, facilities and social encouragement for people to develop their minds, learning would be a major activity, but I believe it would need to be a balanced training, of hand and heart as well as mind.

It is in the lack of such a balance that I see the major weakness of our present educational system. Too great an emphasis is laid on academic knowledge, and not enough on creativity and originality. University students, encouraged to reproduce from memory enormous quantities of written material, have been known to commit suicide or have nervous breakdowns because the pressure of their intellectual training has not been balanced by an encouragement to use their hands in creative skills. Sports have sometimes been offered as an 'approved' outlet, but for those without the physical stamina or interest in competitive sports, much greater satisfaction, sanity and pleasure can be found in activities such as stamp-collecting, pottery, painting, acting, writing poetry, playing musical instruments, doing-it-them-selves, needlework or making a garden. These activities would be given recognition for their self-fulfilling and therapeutic properties in a Creative Society and also given encouragement by means of classes to improve skill, opportunities to exhibit, inter-community competitions, and so on.

What is life for?

I see the goal of a Creative Society as being the finding of satisfaction and self-fulfilment by as many human beings in the world as possible, whether they prefer comfort or adventure, isolation or gregariousness, travelling or staying still, ordered regularity or infinite variety. With this much freedom of choice, there should be incentive for most men and women to accept the social system and be responsible towards it, so that crime and destruction might be almost eliminated, at least to the point where civic order could be maintained by an English-style police force rather than armies or Civil Guards or a Ton-ton Macut. Meanwhile, group aggression could find outlets in contests, and race aggression in trying to find the best answer to the age-old question 'What is life for?'

This question, in fact, would be the focal educational concept of a Creative Society and world-wide publicity and encouragement would be given to all ideas and inventions which added to knowledge that would benefit the human race by improving their way of life mentally, emotionally or physically. Open-ended work in solving technological problems to which there are many possible answers is already being introduced in schools, but we have a long way to go before every student develops to the full his powers of producing all kinds of original solutions to a wide variety of problems as part of his normal education.

A difficulty here might be in finding enough teachers, since the power to communicate interest and enthusiasm for knowledge to other people needs innate qualities which can be trained, but not wholly taught. However, teachers could be helped by machines, some of which are, of course, already in use, and so be able to teach successfully very large classes.

We might imagine, for instance, a classroom around the year 2000, where each of 200 students has his or her own television screen and personal controls that allow the running through of the lesson-film at the rate that best suits the individual: a lesson-film that could include or skip repeats and more detailed information. In such a classroom, the human lecturer would spend, say, half-hour periods with small seminar groups of not more than ten or a dozen students at a time, answering their questions and planning the written work they would do on the subject in their 'homework' or 'private study' period.

This sort of teaching method, although unsuitable for the smallest children, who need the motherlike reality of talking to and even touching their teacher (as many a bruised infant-school instructress can testify), would probably work efficiently for normal children from eight years old upwards and also for adults, for whom such methods are even now being used for the Open University.

This machine aid would make education less expensive to the state, and less expense, in turn, would mean that people might take a longer time to absorb academic knowledge, interspersing such study with manual skills and creative work or doing practical work in their particular field. Primary schools would probably be most usefully sited within individual communities, near to children's homes, but senior schools and universities might form part of a centre-city or intercommunity complex where a group of buildings of particular social and architectural interest might make a focal point for civic pride and sightseeing. Such a centre could also include fountains, gardens and cafés, where people could go to sit out – on the pavements, when the climate was right, or else under transparent domes to watch the world go by. Other buildings in this type of area might include an art gallery, a library, a museum, theatres for professional and amateur dramatic performances, cinemas, skating-rinks, civic offices and meeting halls.

Houses in a Creative Society, however varied in plan and architectural style, would have as a common factor that each would be large enough to allow every member of the household to have space to indulge his or her hobby; which would probably, of course, include gardening, so that streets might be brightened by flowering trees and climbing plants trailing over garden walls or down from apartment roof-gardens. No block of apartments, however, would be more than four storeys high and outlying neighbourhoods would be saved from drab, dead-end suburban uniformity by being interspersed with their own service buildings such as shops, schools, craft centres, dance and meeting halls, swimming baths and perhaps even the occasional high office block. Above all these buildings, the parks, the streets, the squares, would run a noiseless monorail, graceful and glittering on high columns, linking streets at half-mile intervals with community focal points or city centres (see chapter 6).

Apart from private gardens, public parks and other play-spaces within the communities, land would be made available, wherever possible, to surround cities with a countryside for walking, boating, picnicking or climbing. Where a natural seashore or mountainside existed this, of course, would need no help from man, but where the only land that could be spared from agriculture was flat or waterless or derelict, young people might work together to landscape this as a community countryside, on the lines of the scheme already proposed for the Lea Valley.

It has been said that people who like to live in an agricultural community, or in isolation, are seeking, even today, a way of life that is no longer valid. This, like the predictions about over-population, I believe to be untrue. With new methods of irrigation and climate control (see chapter 7) far wider areas of crop-growing countryside could become tolerable for living in and might offer the most comfortable environment, not only for the misogynist or the nature-lover, but also for the worker who prefers non-intellectual work. Also, to make the best long-term use of land, a much larger proportion of people must work on it at present in the developed countries.

Farm communities have already been proved successful in offering people who are mentally retarded the most fulfilled life possible in terms of companionship, interest and a sense of being useful and, with automatic machines to do the drudgery of farmwork, humans in such communities would need only to tend animals and dispatch farm produce to the towns. Elsewhere, however, in the labour-surplus conditions that would exist in a Creative Society, there must be some return to small fields, mixed farms and crop rotation, with the intention of growing food under 'natural' conditions and keeping the land in good heart for generations to come.

Information about weather could be sent to remote farm communities by video-phone from the nearest city weather station, where world weather-computers could make available reasonably accurate long- and short-term forecasts.

Computers and communications in the Creative Society

At present the computer is an instrument very much inferior to the human brain. Not only does the human brain have about 1,000 times as many memory units (called neurons) as the largest computer made so far, but also each neuron has interconnections to some 10,000 other neurons, which means that the number of interconnections in the brain is some five million times as many as the largest computer. The computer works essentially with a single chain in series, although extremely fast. It may be the strengthening of certain interconnectors and the weakening of others that constitutes our learning process and enables us to remember many thousands of words in a language, or sometimes in several languages, and their meanings in different contexts.

The biggest help in integrating the world population of the Creative Society would be the overcoming of language barriers. If we could develop computers with a system of interconnections as complex as the human brain, we might make 'instant translators'. However, this is unlikely to be achieved mechanically and would only be feasible if interconnections could be 'grown' through some random chemical process.

The best equivalent achievable by about the year 2000 would probably be a small computer, carriable in a knapsack, into which an individual could speak in his own language and have his words translated into a universal code in which each word had only one meaning. The stranger to whom he wished to speak would then only have to connect his own national-language computer to the first speaker's computer to hear a reasonably clear translation of what had been said to him. Inevitably, the international code, which would have to be compiled by world experts in semantics, would be emotionally sterile, in the same way that no video-phone meeting could ever really substitute for people meeting each other and eating together and getting to know each other. However, the computers would achieve a better understanding than sign-language, especially in conveying scientific or technological information or the basic needs of ordinary life.

Computers will also be useful in a Creative Society for shopping. Shops could have a filmed selection of all their comparable goods which could be shown to customers on demand by video-phone. Each item would have its own code-number and the shopper-by-video-phone could make a note of all the items which interested him or her and either then visit the shop to inspect the goods more closely or else, particularly with food or household goods, dictate a list of the code numbers to the store, where a computer would check the customer's credit card, organize the collection of all the ordered items into one container, and dispatch the order by way of the community transport system.

This goods transport system would run underground. In the Creative Society, everything possible would be done to keep the streets for pedestrians, and the only above-ground traffic would be an occasional mechanized trolley, a 'taxi' trolley carrying a long-distance traveller with heavy luggage to take with him (see chapter 6), or a van delivering goods too large to go into a cylindrical container 30 cm in diameter and $1\frac{1}{2}$ m long. This cylinder could have hemispherical ends and be split longitudinally for loading. The canister, when loaded, could have a series of dials in its side, turned and locked in a position corresponding to the number representing the postal address of the customer's house.

A network of branching service tubes could run like gas or water pipes under all the buildings in a community and the canisters would travel through this, either along belts or else by means of the sort of pneumatic conveyor tube used for many years to take bills and cash to and from shop accounts departments. In this second method of propulsion, pressurized air would be fed to a region along the bottom of the conveyor tube and separated from it by a plate. The canisters would be floated on an air cushion from small flaps in the plate which would only open when a canister was over them. Once friction had been eliminated, a small forward force produced by air pressure behind the canisters could move them forward at the required speed, which might be 10 km per hour in a main distribution tube and 4 km per hour in branches and sub-branches. Each section in the code-number 'address' fixed to the canister would select the direction the canister would take at any branch-point.

Rubbish could be dealt with by the same system. It would be essential to re-use as much discarded material as possible, and in a way which did not pollute or disfigure the environment at any stage, so every house would have, say, five refuse doors built into the refuse-room or kitchen floor, each one openable by a foot-pedal and feeding into a refuse canister identical to those used for goods delivery except in their method of opening. For refuse, the canister would hinge at one end so that canisters could stand in a vertical position under their access doors, rather like taller, narrower versions of the present-day dustbin. One canister would be for compostible food refuse; one for reconstitutable paper; one for plastics materials; one for metals, broken glass and pottery; and one for uneaten cooked food and other burnable rubbish.

When any one of the canisters was full, it could be closed and automatically released into the goods-transport service tube, already addressed with the label that would direct it to the right department of the community waste-disposal service. Perhaps the community compost-nursery could exchange each canister of new compost-material sent by a household for another of well-rotted compost for use in the family's garden!

The burnable rubbish might go directly to a community heating-boiler which would then supply central heating, hot water and electricity for every building in the community. This combustible material would not, of course, be enough to provide the only fuel for the community heating boiler and possible developments in the efficiency of other power production will be discussed in chapter 8.

The refuse canister for broken hardware could go to a sorting machine which would automatically sort the ferrous metals magnetically and send them to be melted down, and separate the brass, aluminium, broken glass and ceramics by a multiple density flotation separator, similar to those used at present to separate coal and shale at mines. Brass, aluminium and glass could be re-melted and ceramics could be crushed and used as 'grog' for brickmaking.

Plastic waste, by the year 2000, ought to be a comparatively minor problem since, in a Creative Society, non-returnable containers of any kind would certainly be illegal. For such plastic refuse as there is, I hope that experiments now going on to find a bacteria to destroy it will have proved successful, or else that some economic method will have been found of re-using it.

New York City has put forward a packaging tax levied on goods according to the ease with which the packaging can be disposed of or used again, and anti-pollution-minded housewives are removing the surplus wrapping from the goods they buy and leaving it with the shop that sells it. Such people already have a Creative Society outlook.

6

World transport in a Creative Society

Long-distance transport across a united world would always, of course, be most quickly achieved by air. In a Creative Society air travel would be for everyone and so it would have to be made more economical with regard to the use of raw materials (especially fuel) than it is today, as well as safer and more comfortable.

The discomfort of air travel at present, however, lies not so much in the actual flight – which, as everyone knows who travels regularly, is the comparatively relaxing part of an air journey – but in the delays and frustrations encountered before the traveller gets onto the plane and after his aircraft reaches the airport nearest to his final destination. The crawl to and from each city, the queue to weigh-in luggage and get customs clearance, the delays made more disquieting by the constant alarm of Tannoy announcements of other people's flight arrivals and departures, all make air travel exhausting and frustrating.

The journey to and from the city could, I believe, be most comfortably accomplished in a combined transport system which I also see as part of the solution to the whole problem of travelling – a type of trolley-seat that would have the advantages of both public and private transport in that it would enable the user to travel from door to door with the maximum of comfort and the minimum of responsibility without ever being separated from his belongings at any time.

I see this trolley-seat, however, as the fourth stage in an evolution from the present private car.

Weaning mankind from the motor-car

The first stage in this evolution would be merely to remove the danger and poison from the present internal combustion engine so that cars could be designed to meet the specification that they should: (a) minimize the risk of accidents by means of such things as anti-skid tyres and brakes; (b) minimize the damage they can cause to human beings in the event of an accident; (c) minimize engine and exhaust noise; (d) completely burn up their fuel and have an exhaust that discharged at roof level so that the CO_2 in the exhaust would disperse as rapidly as possible. Probably a compressed or liquefied gaseous fuel, such as methane or propane, would have to be used instead of petroleum, because these could be metered equally to all cylinders and there would not be the combustion problems due to liquid droplets; (e) last thirty years to reduce the consumption of raw materials and fuel in manufacturing.

The cost of making cars to this specification would probably add about 20 per cent to present-day prices and would also mean a loss in acceleration, but the gain, of course, would be in safety and freedom from pollution. The extra cost, however, might prompt manufacturers to go ahead quickly to a second stage in car development: getting rid of the internal combustion engine altogether and substituting one of the non-polluting power systems now at an experimental stage.

For example, makers might adopt the type of diesel engine already on the road in a bus in Germany, which has one-fifth of the horse-power normally necessary to give a bus of this type achievable acceleration. This diesel engine runs at a constant speed and a constant power and drives a DC generator which charges batteries that operate electric motors on the wheels. For a few kilometres in the centre of the city, the diesel engine is turned off altogether and the bus is then run on its batteries alone. The batteries can give the necessary acceleration with less than half the horse-power a direct diesel drive would need because they give a very high torque at low revolutions. For the same reason, no clutch or gearbox is necessary and the motors can be directly coupled to the driving wheels. Regenerative braking, too, can help recharge the batteries.

The basic advantages of this system are that the diesel engine is much smaller than a conventional engine and, running at a constant speed and horse-power, can be designed always to give the best possible combustion.

Experimental studies are also going on at the present time on three other kinds of car engine in which combustion is continuous and not intermittent. In the intermittent combustion engines (spark ignition and diesel) there are only a few milliseconds in which combustion has to be completed and every flame has to be separately ignited. In the petrol engine there is the added difficulty of obtaining an equal fraction of the petrol to each cylinder. In a continuous combustion system the flame can be self-stabilizing, that is to say that heat from the flame further along is fed back to ignite the fresh fuel as it enters and there is no difficulty in obtaining complete combustion with a small percentage of excess air. It is also possible to avoid the formation of oxides of nitrogen by keeping the flame cool by extracting heat from it as it burns.

The three continuous combustion engines now being tested are the Stirling cycle, the gas-turbine and the steam-engine. The Stirling cycle engine is a modern development of the old 'hot air engine' with a continuously fired heat exchanger system where the compressed cycling gas is preheated in a regenerative heat exchanger; kept hot as it expands in the power cylinder; cooled in the regenerator heat exchanger at low pressure, and recompressed at low temperature in a cooled cylinder to repeat the cycle. By using hydrogen or helium sealed in at very high pressures as the working fluid, it has been possible to obtain comparable power/weight performance to the internal combustion engine – but this engine is rather elaborate to manufacture.

The gas-turbine is already being installed in lorries of 300 horsepower or more. It is less tiring to drive than a lorry with a conventional engine, has better hill-climbing ability, is lighter, has a simpler gearbox, and does not need a clutch or radiator. Even with an efficient heat exchanger, however, the gas-turbine still uses slightly more fuel than a diesel engine of the same power. Moreover, it is much less practicable to manufacture for the lower horse-powers which would be necessary if pollution was to be minimized and fuel conserved.

Many groups of workers, mostly in the United States, are developing steam cars, and there seems little doubt that this work will produce a commercially viable steam-engine. The steam-engine has superior torque/speed characteristics, that is to say it can pull better at low speeds so that it only needs to have a total power two-thirds to one-half as great as a petrol-engine. Other advantages are that, by using a single-tube flash boiler, only two or three kilogrammes of water are needed, so there is less danger of explosion than with a petrol-engine: also there would be no trouble starting a steam-engine in cold weather, provided that the water had been kept above freezing point, of course.

A steam car has, in fact, already been built which generates steam in fifteen seconds after light-up. All the same, the steam engine may not be developed to a stage where it can be put into commercial production before a third stage is reached in the evolution I foresee between the present private car and a future trolley-seat system. This third stage is a fuel cell which burns liquid fuel with air to produce electricity directly, noiselessly and without any of the fumes or inefficiency of a combustion engine. I believe that such a cell will be successfully developed within the next twenty years and that it might become the power source for town cars, even if a steam-engine was used for intercity journeys.

The multi-purpose trolley-seat

The fuel-cell could, in fact, be used as a power source for special trolley-seats for the elderly or sick or other people who could not, for one reason or another, push their trolley by hand either to a 'train' or to a 'taxi rank' of individual, electrically driven carriages that would be powered either by storage batteries or fuel-cells, and which would carry up to four trolleys with the travellers seated on them.

Before talking about these trolleys in detail, I want to emphasize that I do not see them being used in a Creative Society in the same way that the private car is used in our present society because, as I said in the last chapter, I believe the ideal must be that streets should be kept as free as possible from all but foot traffic. However, everyone could own a trolley, which would have on it a seat and a luggage box. There would be room for more luggage under the seat and the luggage box could be positioned either behind the seat to form a back-rest or in front of the seat to form a leg-rest, so that the seat could become a fully reclining couch. The trolley would have two small front wheels which could be locked to point forward or sideways. At the back, it would have a single wheel on a castor so that, although the unit would normally be pushed forward, it could also be pushed sideways to manœuvre it into a row of seats on a plane or 'train'.

All trolleys would have safety harnesses and would be locked (usually facing backwards) to the floor of trains, planes or individual powered carriages by a high energy absorption plastically deforming steel helix, giving a maximum displacement of one metre. A worktable would be carried on the trolley and this could be fixed in front of the passenger at various heights by steel tubes on both sides of the seat.

This basic trolley would be bought or hired by an individual owner and garaged at his home. The electrically driven carriages, however, would be community-owned, identical and interchangeable. Carriages would have both sides fully openable, the top section a transparent sheet hinged at the roof and the bottom section a steel sheet hinged at floor-level and forming, when it was opened outward and downward, a ramp up which the trolley-seat could be hauled by a cable driven by a motor on the carriage. Their storage batteries would be plugged in and recharged at cab-ranks and rail stations so as to be ready for the next user.

Powered carriages could be either individual, one-, two-, or four-trolley carriages for use as 'cabs' on the streets, or 'trains' boarded at 'stations' and running along a track or overhead monorail 'highway'.

This monorail, already mentioned in chapter 5, would be supported on concrete arches above the streets, a double rail carrying vehicles in both directions. Its stations would be reached from the street by moving platforms, on the principle of an escalator but with steps wide enough to hold several travellers and their trolley-seats at one time. Carriages would hang below the monorail and be monitored by a central computer. The carriages would be supported by two T-shaped hangers hooked inside slots on the bottom of the tubular rails, and air from an electrically driven compressor inside the carriage would be provided with sufficient quantity and pressure to float the two hangers 1 mm above the lower inside surface of the rail. This would eliminate all wheel noise so that the overhead system would be quite silent.

Propulsion would be by the three-phase AC from the conductors, producing a moving magnetic field in the steel tube by means of coils on the hangers which pulled the hangers along. This would constitute the linear motor which has already been shown by Laithwaite to have excellent traction characteristics. An emergency stop could be made by switching off the air supply.

This monorail system, although probably more practicable than a track, would be only one component of the trolley-seat principle. Another component would be battery or fuel-cell driven platform carriages available as self-drive taxis with the ability to carry up to four people each on their trolley-seat. These carriages would have a maximum speed of 50 km per hour and a range of 30 km, so they would be for short distance travel to rail or air terminals only. All four wheels of the carriages might be steerable up to 90° in either direction, so that

5 Portrait busts of his wife and family carved by Professor Thring. The encouragement of craft hobbies would be an essential part of a Creative Society, giving everyone the chance to find a personal satisfaction and self-fulfilment so often missing in people's lives today.

6 A schematic model of the domestic house-working robot. The base would be a four-wheel drive carriage, with wheels having twelve sprung spokes so that the robot could climb stairs. The hand (far right) would be capable of simple grasping and holding movements and would be supported on a jointed arm attached to a fixed pillar (left). It would be guided by a scanning range-finder device on top of the pillar. The machine would incorporate a computer which could be programmed to carry out a wide range of household tasks.

they had powered movement sideways or backwards. The inter-coupling of the motors to give zero slip of wheels under all conditions (including that in which the front wheels only were steered, to take the carriage round a corner) would be carried out electronically with the motors also serving as regenerative brakes, feeding power back into the batteries.

Wheeled carriages would have only two driving controls: the first, a small steering pointer to point the front wheels in the direction the driver wished the vehicle to go; the second, an acceleration pointer, movable from a fully-braked position, through various speeds to a 50 km per hour maximum.

All carriages would need servicing every three months and would carry an electric clock which would show an alarm sign when they were due for servicing. Another indicator would show clearly the contents of the batteries, which could be recharged from the mains at any point where the carriage was parked because the carriage would carry its own rectifier charger.

Travelling with a trolley-seat

When any individual wished to make a journey too far for walking, he would only need to load everything he wanted to take with him into the seat of his trolley, dial for an individual carriage (or wheel his trolley to the nearest carriage rank), hire the carriage by placing his credit card in a slot, and lock his trolley-seat in place on the carriage. He could then use this one-trolley carriage for the whole of a short journey, or he could drive it to a 'station', where a larger 'train' carriage would take him along the track or monorail system.

At the station, the one-trolley carriage, being publicly owned, could be abandoned to be hired by a passenger leaving a 'train'. There would therefore probably need to be a human crew at each station to organize the parking, servicing and hiring of carriages, although this might possibly be operated through a central computer with closed loop radio control.

Alternative cross-city transport might be the Battelle Integrator, being studied at the moment. This is a belt which could run con-tinuously at a speed of up to 30 km per hour overground or through tunnels, or a combination of the two, like the present London under-ground system. Because the whole length of the belt could be uniformly filled with people (and here, again, the trolley-seats might be used), the belt can take up to three times as many passengers as a fully-loaded train system where the trains must be kept apart for safety reasons. Because it does not stop at intermediate stations it can take people in less time than a stopping train system, even with a speed considerably lower than the top speed of the trains.

The main difficulty with the Battelle belt, however, lies in speeding up passengers at a station, so that they can easily step onto the belt, and slowing them down again when they want to get off it. A series of belts has been suggested, each going at 2 km per hour faster than the one before, an idea that was put forward in H. G. Wells's *The Sleeper Awakes*, written sixty years ago. Battelle have solved the problem of stepping from one of these belts to another by using an integrator in the form of a series of small platforms onto which passengers step. These platforms carry people slowly towards the main belt and at the same time accelerate in the direction of the belt movement, so that when the passengers reach the belt they are moving alongside it at the same speed. The platforms continue to travel along with the belt for a sufficient distance for ascending passengers to climb on and descending passengers to climb off the belt, then the platforms reverse, slowing down as they move away towards vertical belts which come up to form sides to the horizontal belt when the belt is not passing a station. These side belts sink down to let passengers off and the integrator platforms cross underneath the horizontal belt and come up on the other side to repeat their manœuvre in reverse.

Outside a community or city, trolley-seats might travel on special long-distance 'trains' powered by steam engines. An alternative form of propulsion might be a 120 km per hour moving magnetic field device placed under a motorway, with acceleration and deceleration branch points. For a magnetic motorway, a special electric carriage with large wheels and high-speed springing would have to be made available on hire. This could have a thirty-kilometre battery drive, like the city 'taxis', but also an electromagnet, or even a permanent magnet, with poles close to the ground at the front and rear. After being driven to the nearest branch point adjoining the motorway, this carriage would be automatically accelerated to motorway traffic speed and slotted into the traffic stream when a gap occurred in the line of vehicles. The driver could then sit back in his trolley-seat and read or look out of the transparent 'roof' until his carriage, travelling at identical speed with all the other carriages, reached the branch point he had previously indicated on his time-coded secondary electromagnet. Here the carriage would be automatically branched off and slowed down to the 'local' 50 km per hour.

Another alternative intercity transport system would be a larger version of the intercommunity monorail. Across country, monorail 'trains' could be driverless and reach speeds of 300 km per hour between stops which would be perhaps 100 km or more apart. This would mean that a journey between, say, London and Glasgow city centres would take only about two hours. Travel at this speed would be practically noiseless as the linear motor would be silent and the air bearing would only make a slight hissing sound. A central computer control system could keep each 'train' clear of the next and allow a frequent service.

Air transport

A monorail system could also serve airports. A main monorail would meet special airport 'trains' at junctions, where airline passengers and their trolley-seats could transfer and be beyond the 'customs' barrier, all luggage weighing and formalities being carried out on the way to the airport.

Airports could then consist of concrete platforms, perhaps built out into the sea or a lake, with no obstructions above ground except for a single mast carrying television cameras pointing in all directions, and a radar scanner. Planes could be parked at points on the platform, which could have up to six runways, and the monorail transport carriages could 'dock' in tunnels below the runways. When the passengers arrived in these tunnels, they could take their trolley-seats off the monorail carriage, push them to their correct plane loading-bay, be raised on a platform-lift to the side of the plane and push their trolley-seats into position within its fuselage.

In this way, each individual would have brought his seat and luggage from his own home right into the plane which would fly him across the world, where he would be able to convey his trolley-seat by exactly the same monorail, carriage or hand-propelled system to the home or hotel where he was proposing to stay.

Since luggage would all be under its owner's seat, airplanes would not need a separate luggage compartment and a 1,000 seater plane might have three decks each with 34 rows of ten seats on each deck.

Even 5,000 seater planes might be possible, using this system, and therefore air travel might be made cheap enough for it to come within the financial reach of everyone. Fewer, larger planes would make landing and taking off safer; less fuel would be used per passenger; and airlines would be able to afford to spend extra money on such safety devices as infra-red viewing, sonar, and radar for landing in foggy weather.

It might, further, even be possible for planes, even the 1,000 seater planes, to take off directly from city centres, without noise and at the same time with a smaller engine than present-day conventional aircraft. This would be achieved by having a hollow steel tube, split at the underside and sufficiently strongly supported on pylons to carry the full loaded weight of the plane. Passengers would be taken up by lift to the plane, which would be suspended by electromagnets and hooks 100 metres above ground-level in the very centre of a city. The plane would hang from a carriage supported on air bearings on a rail along which the carriage could be accelerated by linear electric motor to 1,000 km per hour, carrying the plane up the rail. At the end of the rail, the plane would be released and would climb to its full flight level using conventional jet-engines for this purpose and achieving a height of 4,000 m in a distance of about 10 km.

Incoming planes could land at an airfield that was outside the city. When a plane had landed and been refuelled, it could travel to the centre-city terminal at 200 km per hour, noiselessly and with electric drive power, ready to deposit its incoming passengers, collect outgoing passengers and take off again in the manner I have described above.

This idea could be extended again to include the development of a combined rail and plane system for travel within any one country or continent; the basic units being a monorail with carriers from which passenger-loaded fuselages could be hung and conveyed at 160 km per hour. A passenger for any given flight could board his fuselage at a town-centre terminal and travel by monorail to the launching site. At the launching site, all arriving fuselages would be put into winged cradles with 960 km per hour air propulsion systems. At this point, too, a human pilot would enter the cockpit. The completed 'plane', comprising the fuselage with its wings, would then be hung from a carrier on an inclined launching rail two miles long, where it would be silently accelerated to full speed by the linear motor on the carrier and released

1,000 feet above ground-level. During this period the winged cradle's own motors would accelerate from tick-over to full thrust and, on release, would take over from the carrier motor.

When this 'plane' reached its destination, it could land at an airport outside a city where the wings and pilot could be separated from the fuselage and the fuselage transferred, in a few minutes, to a monorail carrier. By monorail, the fuselage could again travel at 160 km per hour to the centre of the arrival city where passengers could alight. Alternatively, a fuselage might leave a landing site, say at Heathrow, London, and deliver passengers to the centres of Reading, Oxford, Birmingham, Manchester, Leeds and Newcastle. This system could, of course, be combined with the trolley-seat system already described.

The flight unit, the wings, engines and fuel tanks could be serviced, refuelled and checked at the landing airport and then sent either by monorail to a centre-city launching site or to an intercity airport with transfer bays up to ten storeys high, to save ground space. The flight units would be interchangeable for any fuselage of one of three sizes: to carry 50, 200 or 1,000 passengers. The separation of the launching system from the landing sites would mean that planes could be launched safely every minute, or even half-minute. Landing could be fully-automatic blind landing, based on sonar beams from plane to ground.

These planes would be subsonic, not supersonic, and it would be possible to halve the fuel used by present-day aircraft by reducing the amount of air dragged forward with the wings. This could be done by putting rubber belts round the wings to cause the surface to move backwards or by having three layers of small vanes along the upper and lower surface of the wing at its rear edge. These vanes would be at right angles to the wing and hinged at their front edge so that when they were pushed towards the wing tip the vanes would flap towards the body and thus act as small propellers pushing air backwards. Conversely, when they were pushed towards the body they would flap towards the tip and again push the air backwards. The three rows of vanes would be violently reciprocated 120° out of phase by direct action of double-acting free pistons in internal combustion cylinders, and thus the air which had been picked up by the wing would be pushed backwards and provide thrust instead of drag, as if a whole line of small propellers were placed all along the wing, because the vanes on top of the wing would push the air with a downward component as well as a backward one and the vanes underneath would push the air horizontally backwards. Thus, this wing would provide more lift than a conventional one, as well as considerably less drag.

For ships, too, fuel could be saved by moving the 'skin' of the ship backwards relative to the ship slightly faster than the ship was moving forward. Eighty per cent of the power of a large ship propelled at 30–50 km per hour is used in dragging the sea forward with the ship – skin friction. If, therefore, the skin of the ship can be moved backwards, not only will it not drag the sea forward and skin friction will be eliminated, but also it will be unnecessary to have screws to push some sea backwards to provide thrust, since the backward-moving skin would do this as well.

A ship propelled in this way would need to have a rectangular deck and nearly vertical sides, bows and stern. Two rubber belts, each covering half the width of the ship, would run round rollers above water-level at the bows and stern so that the outside surface of the belt ran down the bow plane, which would be inclined at 45° to the vertical, and then along the bottom of the hull and up the stern, which would have a similar incline to that of the bow.

Two belts would be necessary for this system so that steering could be effected by running each belt at a different speed. These belts would be housed in compartments on the outside of the side of the hull, air being blown into the compartments with sufficient pressure both to keep water out and to allow some air to escape at the edges to form an air bearing.

Such a ship would be able to crawl up a gently sloping beach or concrete ramp, right out of the water, because the air-bearing surface of the belt would carry the weight. The sides of the ship could, on shore, be let down so that lorries could run up to, or even into, the hold to unload cargo.

Another method of carrying at least up to 200 tons of goods could be by airship. Airships could be filled with helium and need only a fraction of the fuel used by a plane carrying the same load. Such airships might be 300 m long, 60 m in diameter, and fly at a height of 900–1,200 m, travelling at speeds of 180 km per hour. At this speed, goods could be taken from London to Australia in 100 hours – or passengers could find a pleasant means of cruising for relaxation.

7

Food production in a Creative Society

A first step towards ending our aggressive, competitive society and achieving a Creative Society could, perhaps, most successfully be the ending of hunger and malnutrition in the world. For this, it would be essential for the richer countries to find the way to give real help to the poorer ones – that is to say the sort of help that would enable them to help themselves.

So far all the efforts that have been made to this end have been unsuccessful because, in spite of them, the gap between the standards of living in the under-developed countries has widened within the last half century. There are many reasons for this, the most important being the fact that both governments and businessmen in the industrialized countries have only given help to the poorer countries for selfish reasons. Ordinary idealistic people could put pressure on their governments, and the governments, in turn, could join with, and put pressure on, business organizations to provide help where and when it was of greatest benefit – not to themselves, but to the receiving country.

But as well as 'where' and 'when', 'how' help was given would need to be carefully considered. It might do more harm than good, for example, to send sophisticated heavy industry, or advanced labour-saving farm machinery, to an area where labour was so plentiful that the same job could be done more effectively by traditional handtools. Rather, a special kind of technology is needed, using the latest techniques and materials to deal with specific, local problems. The Intermediate Technology Development Group Ltd, in London, is already beginning to do this, mainly by finding out which tools and devices already on the market could be of greatest value – even if these are handtools, or tools to be powered by animals or steam-engines operating on local fuel.

Although we have envisaged world population doubling by the end

73

of the century, and must face the fact that the biggest increase will come in the under-developed countries, there need not necessarily be any shortage of nourishment. If the land that is at a convenient height above sea-level and has adequate rainfall can be fully cultivated, properly fertilized and irrigated by water controlled through a system of channels, dams and reservoirs, enough food could be grown to feed ten times the present world population. Chemical fertilizers, such as ammonium sulphate, put the necessary nitrogen into the ground: although it is now realized that the humus will be taken out of the soil in time unless a certain amount of composting is carried out, by ploughing back stalks, rotating crops and letting animals graze the land, and using human manure from cities.

In many parts of the world, however, the main food problem is the shortage of protein in the available diet. Solutions are being found in defatted soyabean flour and protein concentrate, which is extracted from leaves and green material, such as peapods. Plants can give a yield of protein per acre many times that of grazing animals. In fact, by the year 2000 animal meat may have become so uneconomical to produce as a regular source of protein that it will be eaten only in small quantities, as a condiment, as the Chinese use it now.

A small device is already available which can be fixed to a Landrover, from which it derives its power, to extract the protein from 100 kg per hour of vegetable matter. This vegetable protein can be made interesting to eat by such very simple means as putting a layer of it inside a split banana.

Some scientists have hailed chlorella, grown in water in greenhouses, as the food of the future; but this would be expensive in terms of buildings, and plants grown in open fields can give an equal return in organic matter per hectare per year, provided that water and sun are available – which might be guaranteed by the climate control methods I shall be describing later in this chapter.

A major oil company has also produced a nourishing protein from a bland paraffin wax fermented by yeasts and bacteria, and it has been estimated that 3 per cent of the present world petroleum output could produce twenty million tons of pure protein a year.

Water and climate control

Over three thousand years ago, crops were grown in what is now the Negev desert by the control of night dew. A great pit was filled with stones and the dew collected in the pit and could be run off to irrigate a small belt of land near by. In many parts of the world there would be sufficient dew and rainfall to provide water for growing food if (as now happens under natural conditions) this water did not evaporate in the hot daytime sunshine or else drain away before it can be used, often into ground where it picks up salts and becomes brackish.

Too rapid evaporation of this kind could be reduced by establishing ground cover, first of all by man-made screening units while trees and grass were grown, and then by the shade of the trees, when other crops than grass could be planted. In a Creative Society system, where long-term advantages to people would outweigh quick profitability, not-immediately-profitable dams and irrigation channels could also be built, although channels and reservoirs would need to be constructed, in future, to have some means of flushing out and using the valuable silt that accumulates inside them.

But there is already available one method for using modern materials to solve the age-old problem of providing drinking water in hot regions where it only rains for a few days of the year. This method uses a butyl rubber sheet to line a shallow conical hollow or collecting area. In the centre, a deep cylindrical hole is dug and the sides of this hole are lined with bags filled with soil or sand and covered with another butyl sheet to reduce evaporation. In the rainy season the cone collects all the rain falling on it, the rain running down into the central pit, which acts as a storage well for the rest of the year.

Studies have already started, too, on a system in which solar energy is used to raise water a few metres from a well for irrigation purposes. This device is for use in places where the well-water, derived originally from rain, stays free from excessive salt. The method of raising it to ground-level is based on the coffee-percolator principle where the steam bubbles lighten the column of liquid so that it rises. A large tank, on the surface of the land to be irrigated, is filled with water above which air is trapped. The lid of this tank consists of three layers of pressure-tight plastic sheeting which transmit sunlight but prevent low-temperature heat from escaping. When the pressure in this absorber rises sufficiently, the mixture of steam and air flows down a pipe into the bottom of a container under the surface of the water in the well and blows the water up a pipe at the top of the container into the irrigation channel. When the container is empty, a flap valve opens and lets in more water. This is a practical use of solar energy since, if irrigation is needed at all, there will necessarily be plenty of sunlight.

No method has yet been invented to prevent rainfall and dew soaking too deeply into the ground, but in sandy deserts this might be done by having a specially designed plough which could be towed along with its blade two metres under the surface. At the same time, the ploughing machine would unroll a thin sheet of plastic two metres wide from a roll housed in the plough nose. A whole area would thus be made almost impervious at a two-metre depth, using overlapping plastic sheets. An alternative method would be to inject a layer of paraffin wax at the required depth.

Where brackish water is available in sufficient quantities, there are several methods by which it might be pumped to the surface and made sweet. Perhaps the most promising method is reversed osmosis. Osmosis is the process whereby a special membrane allows pure water to pass through into a concentrated salt solution until the pressure is very much higher on the salt side than on the pure water side. Reversed osmosis is based on the discovery that by applying a still higher pressure by a pump to the salty side, pure water can be forced through the membrane, leaving the salt behind. It is now possible to make such membranes on a large scale and use them to line steel tubes pierced with many small holes. Hundreds of these steel tubes can then be built to form a plant that will provide several tons of irrigation water each day. Such a plant, in fact, has now been planned to provide all the water necessary to support an agricultural community in regions of the Negev desert where rain falls every two or three years, and even then runs into underground reservoirs where it picks up too much salt to be directly usable.

If salt can be removed, then sea-water, too, can be used for irrigation, only here the best method of purification is more likely to be by distillation because of the very high salt content. Various ingenious devices exist whereby the latent heat of evaporation (540 kcals/kg or 0·63 kwh/kg) can be used several times over (multiple-effect evaporation), but such heat can only be produced by burning fuels, and unless there happened to be, say, a good deal of woody by-product from the agricultural process in need of irrigation, it would be much too expensive to produce an adequate fuel-heated water supply.

Many schemes have been put forward employing nuclear fission reactors to distil sea-water. The reactors primarily make electricity and use up their lower grade heat energy for multiple-effect evaporation.

However, the huge capital cost of such a system makes it only feasible where there is a good market for the electricity, such as a big city with an associated heavy industrial complex.

There is, however, one source of heat which can be used economically to distil sea-water for agricultural irrigation: nature's basic source, the sun. Practically all our rainwater comes from the seas and all we have to do is to learn how to control a distillation process. Probably the most practical method will prove to be that of pumping sea-water through a large pipe into the desert, where it would flow into one end of a series of long, plastic-lined troughs, say 10 m wide and 2 km long, running across the land to be irrigated from east to west. These troughs would be spaced 30 m apart and the ground between them would be watered and used to grow crops. The troughs would have three channels, the side ones being only a few centimetres wide. The centre channel would carry the incoming salt-water. All three channels together would be covered by a half-cylindrical thin plastic sheet held in shape by a small air-blower which would put a slight excess air pressure inside it, sufficient to balance its weight.

The solar radiation would pass freely through this covering sheet and would evaporate the water in the central channel which would then rise as steam and, since it could not escape, condense on the inside of the cover and run down its sides into the two outer channels, from which there would be outlets.

This system could be combined with the method already described of laying plastic sheeting two metres down under the soil to stop the precious water soaking too deeply for the crop roots. Where the crop was cabbages or other similar leaf vegetable, the surface of the ground could be covered with white plastic with holes left in it through which the vegetables could grow. This white plastic would cut down the surface evaporation of moisture. Trees, too, might be grown in such an area to encourage dew and rainfall or, alternatively, black bitumen might be painted over some 100 sq km of ground.

This revolutionary proposal, which is now being studied, would work on the theory that sunlight falling on a black, absorbent surface would raise its temperature 20° C above the temperature of the surrounding land. This would cause a rising column of hot air which would lift the rainclouds to such a height that they would discharge their rain inland from the bitumen strip, in the same way that rainclouds break and water the valleys below a mountain range. It is estimated that up to 0·7 metres of additional rainfall could be produced over an area two to three times the size of the area coated with bitumen.

Another possibility is to build an artificial 'mountain range' using a long nylon net pegged down at the edges and held up in the centre by hydrogen-filled bags.

Mechanical farming, including economical transport for food without roads or rails

Much of the land that could be made available for food growing if it were levelled, fertilized or irrigated has the further disincentive to developers at present that it is in a part of the world where there are no roads. Road building or, alternatively, air transport for farmers, farm machinery and harvested crops might make the whole project uneconomical, but soon a machine will be available which can carry five-ton loads at speeds up to 30 km per hour across the roughest country, even swimming or fording deep rivers.

The 'mechanical elephant' or, more accurately, the giant centipede, will have some thirty feet, fifteen a side, on the ground at any one time. These feet, on sprung legs two metres long, will have a movement like that of a tracked vehicle, except that the separate legs, placed on the ground in front and staying stationary as the full seven-metre length of the vehicle passes over them, will enable the 'elephant' to stride over obstacles and to climb over vertical walls 1½ m high or up hillsides, provided, that is, that the total slope does not exceed 40°. The machine will also have a hydraulic balancing system which will hold the body stable and horizontal when it is moving along a sideways slope up to 30°. The width of the vehicle (five metres) will always ensure that the weight can be kept well inside the legs.

This machine will be able to 'swim' rivers because the 'body' will have a watertight hull and the legs will have flat plates on them that will act like paddles. In a river, the same movement the vehicle makes to 'walk' on land will propel it through the water. When, occasionally, the machine might have to be used on a road surface, however, hard rubber soles would be put on its flat feet so that, unlike a steel caterpillar track, it would do no damage.

The 'elephant' would have a hydraulic hoist, so that it could load and unload containers up to two tons. It would be able to load up at special terminals, collecting goods from lorries, ships or airships; take its load hundreds of kilometres across all types of country, including mountain passes; and bring back local produce to the terminal. Unlike a helicopter or a hovercraft, it would not use much fuel per ton per mile – little more than a heavy lorry.

The same principle of separately sprung legs with solid feet could be used in two other applications in connection with agriculture. When a conventional farm tractor is used on heavy clay soil, its rubber-tyred wheels compact the soil, which prevents moisture and air flowing through it. Therefore, at present, tyred wheels often have to be replaced by steel wheels with spikes or narrow strip cages. This is a laborious job, especially as the tyred wheels have to be put back again whenever it is necessary to drive the tractor on a surfaced road.

A wheel with 20 sprung spokes, each with a flat rubber foot 40 cm long and 5 cm wide, would be suitable for both heavy soil and for roads, and would have the further advantage that the tractor would be firmly supported at its maximum width so that it would be much less likely to overturn sideways than a tractor with rubber tyres.

In ploughing, the real objective is to aerate the soil and the operation of turning the topsoil upside down has often been found to be undesirable, especially if it has brought to the top clay that has lacked enough humus for growing seed. Thus, a device which could punch a large number of holes, say 15 cm deep into the ground, rather as a gardener aerates a lawn with a fork, might in many cases be preferable to the conventional plough and take much less power. A machine which could do this might be made about five metres long and have two caterpillar tracks of steel plates studded with spikes of the required length. The plates could be two metres long and half a metre wide and could move as endless belts with hinges between them under the engine and the body. The plates could pass round hexagonal rollers at each end, the sides of the hexagon being equal to the width of the plates. The rollers would be driven by the engine and the plough would be steered by driving the rollers at different speeds. The lower track would run on rails fixed to the body with small rollers at the corners of each plate, but these rails would be bent to be lower in the centre than at the ends by a height equal to the length of the spikes. Thus, as the plates left the front roller, the spikes would steadily pierce the ground, being withdrawn as the plate came to the back roller.

This would give an essentially vertical piercing action and withdrawal but at the same time, since the front and rear could move sideways when the two tracks were running at different speeds, it would be easy to steer the 'plough', which could also be used for planting if it was adjusted to drop seeds through hollow tubes into holes which would, however, need to be less deep than the aeration holes.

Mechanized farming

There will probably always be regions of the earth where crops are grown in large quantities but where the labour available is in short supply. An example of this is the Canadian Prairies. Here, it would be helpful for one man to be able to control machines that would do all the work automatically. This might be achieved by a combination of telechirics and robotics.

The operator could be in control of, say, several tractors, giving them instructions by radio and following their progress on television screens. From a console, or desk, he could instruct any individual tractor to pull a machine round a field, every time following a given pattern of movement but displacing by exactly one machine width. The first pattern of movement would probably have to be set by steering manually, although even this manual steering would be done by remote control. It might be possible, however, eventually, for machines to set their own patterns following a programmed 'map' and using four radio beams to locate their position in relation to the field. Once the tractor had been instructed to do its job, it would need no further guidance, 'seeing' its way by means of focused photocell 'eyes' on a bar in front of it just above the level of the ground or crop so that it could detect the difference in level or colour it had produced on its previous round. It would probably steer itself round a field more accurately than a human driver, since the human driver always sits a long way above the row he is following.

By using submarine tractors, exactly the same system of armchair control could be used at the bottom of the sea, so that man might, in time, farm the continental shelves of the world, planting not to feed himself, directly, but to feed fish which he would then catch and eat.

However, I shall talk about working at the bottom of the sea in more detail in the next chapter.

8

Paid work in a Creative Society

I have written in chapter 5 that office work would still be necessary, even in an automated society. I said then:

> Although machines could be designed to do all the drudgery and dangerous work in the world, human technical skill and intelligence would still be necessary for maintenance, organization, creativity and any job where human emotion, such as sympathy or enthusiasm, was an essential ingredient of the work. This last would include teaching, caring for the sick and elderly, and every aspect of public relations, from diplomacy to salesmanship.
>
> Experience would have to show, however, how much of the work still needed by society would have to be done at set hours and in exchange for money and how much could be done on a voluntary basis in exchange for honour within the community.

Office work would obviously still need a monetary incentive to persuade people to do it, even though, as I also said in chapter 5, some office work might be done in people's own homes, helped by a video-phone link to company centres. Another useful piece of office equipment which might be developed by the year 2000 and which would be useful both for business activities or for leisure-time creative writing, would be a dictation typewriter. This might be made to type out words as fast as its user could speak them into it, but it would probably need too big a computer to spell English correctly because we have too many different ways of spelling the same sound, and so it would have a phonetic spelling. The typewriter would not be able to comprehend the context fast enough to choose the correct spelling. Russian, Italian or German might more feasibly be spelt correctly, since these languages are fairly phonetic. For English, we should either have to learn to read a machine's 'pidgin' or else give the script to a human secretary for translation and correct presentation.

Such work would represent a mild drudgery to the secretary, but not the sort of monotony to be met with in factories today. On the production side, machines could very well take over all repetitive work, leaving human beings to oversee, design and maintain the machines. Even these skills could be computer- or machine-assisted. When the human beings in a research and development group, for instance, wanted to try out a new idea, they would only have to lay down the design principles and make rough sketches and leave a computer to make detailed drawings which humans could check and assess and correct and send back to the machine again. When the humans finally approved the computer's design, especially with regard to such things as strength, dynamic vibration effects and fluid flow patterns, the computer could convert the design drawing into magnetic-tape instructions for production machines. Humans, however, would probably have to assemble and test the parts for the first experimental prototype so that they could tell the computers to make modifications in the design of the tapes until the optimum design solution was found. After this, the computer would organize production and run off a set of permanent records for the manufacturing of all components.

There will probably be two basic types of factory in the future. The first will produce many millions of identical objects, or a steady flow of electricity, or cement, or refined oil, and the second will manufacture small runs of, say, ten products to 100,000. Below a ten-product output, there would be a need for human handcraftsmen: people who could make individual craft objects with a specialist skill that would be the more fully appreciated in a society where many people would make craft-objects in their leisure time.

For mass-production, on a steady-flow level, factories could be almost fully automated in so far that processes would be directly controlled by a single central computer, and the whole factory would be designed and laid out so that all materials were moved automatically and assembly and testing done on the line. For example, a motor-car works would consist of bays where all components were constructed, assembled and fully tested, fed from raw materials delivered to the factory by automatic railways running inside concrete tubes. From each construction bay, the components would pass on overhead delivery lines to the main assembly line where all the parts could be fitted onto the chassis by

7 Working model of a table-clearing machine designed to test the present-day feasibility of principles required for the house-working robot and other machines. The model has one 'sight' and two 'touch' sensors which enable the mechanical arm to pick up objects and place them on the rotating, clearing tray on top of the machine.

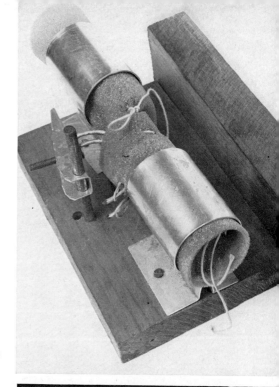

8 Large-scale model of an automatic surgical stitching machine currently being developed to achieve rapid joining of small arteries and nerve sheaths. The machine's speed (five double-loop stitches simultaneously) and the possibility of joining arteries of less than one millimeter diameter, could lead to successful reattachment of severed fingers and limbs.

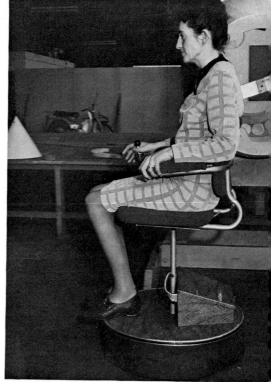

9 Engineers can develop machines to give mobility to people suffering from crippling diseases. This prototype of a mobile seat is capable of moving forwards, backwards and sideways and is controlled by a switch which is pushed in the direction in which the sitter wants to go.

a different machine, especially designed to fit the particular part. The finished car would, of course, be designed with much greater freedom to fill its role as a safe, pollution-free, long-lasting transport device, because manufacturing and assembly would not be limited by the ability of a man's hands to hold a tool or a paint-sprayer, particularly in an awkward position.

Machines would probably do the assembly work more reliably than men. The computer would watch production and inform a human works manager and maintenance crew of any testing rejects or hold-ups on production or assembly.

In a 'small run' factory there would probably be numerically controlled machine tools, some of which are already in use even today. With these, a punched card or magnetic tape is prepared from a drawing by a computer, and then the punched card or magnetic tape controls all the movements of the tool, which produces the designed shapes from blanks or from bar stock. At the moment, this method of production is inferior to skilled human craftsmen in so far that it cannot check by measurement the exact dimensions of the metal left at various stages of the process. However, a flying micrometer has already been developed using a laser beam to measure accurately the diameter or any other overall dimension while the cutting is going on. An instrument of this type, therefore, could be combined with the numerical control system to produce exactly specified dimensions, no matter what variations were met with in the surface hardness of a casting to be cut, or in tool wear.

The grouping together of a set of machine tools so that each one can be fully occupied automatically, and without human supervision, to do its particular work throughout a long sequence of machine operations has already been achieved. This is called System 24. At the moment, System 24 relies on girls, working only in the daytime, placing aluminium blanks on pallets in such a position that they will feed accurately into the machine. The girls' work, however, could in time be carried out by industrial robots, working blind at first, by touch only, to find the blanks in a bin and orient them and feed them to the machine, having had the correct size and shape fed into its computer 'memory', together with instructions for correct grasping by its 'hand'. Later, however, studies now being carried out in connection with machines reading print indicate that it may well be feasible for an industrial robot to see by 'eye', or a pair of range-finder eyes on long stalks. Like the Unimate and the Versatran robots, which are already on the market in America, the industrial robot just described would have to be manipulated into its working position by a separate, man-controlled machine. It would have a box-like body and a powerful hand on the end of an arm.

A second robot which might usefully be developed for the factory is a goods transporter which would act as an automatic trolley or fork-lift truck. This would unload lorries, put the goods in the right compartments in the stores (judging the position of each by its label), inform a central computer of the level of stocks and take objects from the stores to the process machines as they were needed. This robot would look like a larger and more powerful version of the domestic robot which will be fully described in chapter 9. It would have a low truck body on four wheels, the two front ones close together on a steering bogey, with all the heavy working motors, batteries etc., below the carrying tray that would form the surface of the body. In front, a central vertical pillar would rise two metres and carry a swivel at the top with 360° vertical axis rotation and 180° horizontal axis rotation: from this swivel could stretch two joints of an arm. These two joints would be, say, one and a half metres long so that the arm would reach three metres from the swivel and have at its end a vice-like hand which could open up to one metre wide and rotate 180° in any of three directions. The jaws of the hand would have chisel edges to push under a package and would contain touch sensors so that they could sense the grip necessary to pick up a package without crushing it.

The goods transporter would have a rangefinder on top and touch sensors in front for locating obstacles. It would be controlled by a central computer by way of a closed loop radio system, and it would have an 'eye' in its 'hand' which would be able to read labels with magnetic printing and also 'see' a suitable path through the factory, avoiding obstacles and locating the object it had been sent to pick up. When it needed to extend its 'hand', it would put out special stabilizing feet on each side, but when it had loaded the needed object, or objects, onto its tray it would fold away its arm and its feet before carrying its load through the factory. It could be made capable of transporting a load up to about a ton in weight.

The 'worker' robot and the 'transporter' robot could both be mass-produced, since each of them could serve in any factory anywhere in the world. An assembly robot, on the other hand, although equally helpful, would be more expensive to develop since it would have to be made in many sizes. One of the smallest might be used to assemble a watch, while one of the largest could assemble trains or aircraft.

Small assembly robots might have a worktable which would be rotated by the machine in any direction. This would be fitted with special clamps to hold the object to be assembled. A mechanical hand would then pick up the base-piece or 'chassis' of the product from a pile and put it the right way up on the worktable where clamps would grip it. The table would rotate to bring to the top the site to which the next component was to be fixed, and another hand would pick the component from the first of a series of bins holding each of the various parts to make the completed product. The 'hand' would hold each part while an assembly device such as a screwdriver or a rivetter or a welder or a soldering iron sealed it into position. At the end of the assembly process, the robot would test the completed product and either reject it or pass it on for packing.

For assembling large objects, the robot would propel itself round the object it was assembling, orienting itself by 'touch' and 'sight'.

The steelworks of the future

Steel and all non-ferrous metals could pass continuously through all the processes from ore and scrap to finished rolled product, in the same way that oil passes through a refinery now. This whole process could be checked and the product analysed continuously, too, by automatic arc spectroscopes at various points along the production line. A computer could receive these analyses and control the fuel input, slag raw material feed, alloying additions, oxygen and air supply. It could also check the tilt of channels and other controls to produce the required succession of so many tons of a certain thickness of sheet, as required by an instructed formula, and change the formula as this proved necessary. The crushed ore concentrate could be pelletized with fine coal and lime, using a little oil as a bond, and this could be fed into a slot a hundred metres long and two metres wide at the top of a ten-metre high shaft kiln. Here it would be blown, with highly preheated air, through tuyeres every two metres along the sides above the narrow channel which would carry the molten iron and slag to one end, where they would be tapped out fully and continuously through two tap-holes, the lower one being for the iron.

This lower taphole would be ten metres above ground-level and the iron would run out through a short, covered channel to the steel refining furnace.

In order to conserve world resources of natural materials, 80 per cent of steel would come from remelted scrap and only 20 per cent from freshly reduced ore. Thus, for every 100 tons from the shaft kiln, 400 tons of scrap could be melted in a scrap-melting sloping kiln fired with oil plus the producer gas from the shaft kiln. The two liquid streams of metal could join together and flow in counter-current to a lime/ alumina slag to be siphoned out in a vacuum degassing syphon. Thence they could go by way of a runner to a dozen continuous casting plants in parallel, and the cast slabs could be bent round to a horizontal direction as they cooled before going through a succession of rollers to produce the final product.

Developments in efficiency of power production

Figure 1 shows in diagrammatic form the known and possible methods of producing mechanical work and electric power from fossil and nuclear fuels and solar energy. We have not yet developed an engineering machine which can convert chemical energy directly into mechanical work (the left-hand arrow on the triangle), but a mechanical muscle will almost certainly be produced within the next thirty years and this will enable a quiet, cool engine to turn the wheels of cars, or to move the legs of the cross-country centipede carriage described in chapter 7.

The problem here, as with all transport engines, is to consume the necessary amount of fuel in a small-volume low-weight engine. The chemical reaction must be oxidation with oxygen from the air, otherwise the system has to carry the second reagent with it, as well as the fuel, as happens in a rocket. However, when we can find a way of distributing liquid fuel and dissolved oxygen into a network of artificial muscle-cells, we will have a system which not only avoids pollution and noise but also uses only a few times as much fuel as our own legs, walking.

The direct link from chemical reaction to electricity (the right-hand side of the triangle) has already been made. All electric batteries achieve this, but they also consume one of the electrodes as fuel so that they have to be thrown away when they are used up. In the fuel cell, on the other hand, the two chemical reagents (fuel and oxidant) are con-

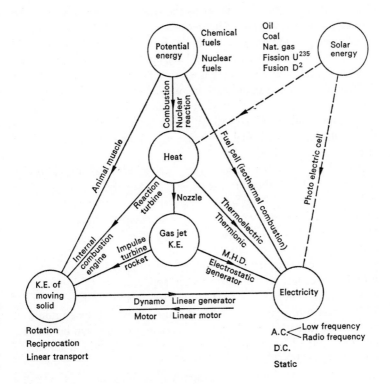

Figure 1 Known and theoretical methods of producing mechanical work from natural power sources. A machine to convert chemical energy directly into mechanical work, as animals do (the left-hand arrow on the triangle), has not yet been developed but this will almost certainly be invented within the next thirty years.

tinuously fed from storage tanks to the two electrodes. The reaction products can then be removed continuously so that electricity is provided as long as the reagents are fed to it. The oxygen/hydrogen fuel cells in space capsules are a successful and well-known example of this.

A good deal of work is being done to try to produce a fuel cell that will run on air and a liquid fuel, because it would then be possible to use such a cell in a car with an electric motor drive on the rear wheels. This again would produce a silent, high efficiency drive that used less than a quarter as much fuel as a conventional car engine, and without any carbon monoxide.

All other methods of producing mechanical work or electricity from chemical fuels first turn the energy into heat, which exacts a price in loss of efficiency. This efficiency loss is the greater the nearer together are the effective upper-working temperature and the effective exhaust temperature of the engine. This is why the steam engine has been designed to operate at higher and higher steam temperatures and pressures in order to try to raise its effective upper-working temperature. It is necessary to use high-vacuum condensers to bring down the exhaust temperature to as near atmospheric temperature as possible. Some years ago, however, a cycle was used in which the combustion heat of the fuel evaporated mercury, because mercury can be usefully evaporated at a higher temperature than water, which is an advantage when it is inadvisable to use a very high pressure. The condensing mercury evaporated water at an intermediate temperature, so that the cycle used two liquid vapours in cascade.

Now work is going on to find a suitable fluid at the lower end of the temperature scale which would enable the steam to be condensed at a pressure around one atmosphere, and evaporate the new fluid at a fairly high pressure. If this could be condensed at just above atmospheric temperature, it would not need the large and expensive high-vacuum condensers that are necessary at the moment.

All these developments have been concerned with small increases above the 40 per cent which is the present best fuel efficiency that can be obtained with a fuel-fired central power station, or else with small reductions in the capital cost of the 500 or 1,000 MW units. No doubt further small improvements will take place along these lines, although big changes are more likely to come in one of the two following ways:

First, there is the possibility of a new cycle being developed which would give overall efficiencies of 50 per cent or more and substantial reductions in cost. Figure 1 indicates the possible cycles, going directly from heat or directed gas jets to electricity without going via mechanical work (such as a rotating shaft) to drive the dynamo. The thermocouple generates electricity by heating a number of thermo-electric junctions directly and then cooling the alternate junctions. This is doomed to a low efficiency because the materials have to be good electrical conductors and this makes them also good heat conductors, so that much more heat is carried along them than is turned into electricity. By using very expensively made semi-conductors, efficiencies up to 13 per cent have been obtained and used to run radios from a flame where reliability is more important than efficiency.

The thermionic generator is similar – two electrodes have a near vacuum between them, one being heated white hot (1500°C or more) and emitting electrons which travel to a cooled electrode against a small electric voltage, so that power is produced. Here thermal radiation limits the efficiency.

The second possible line of development is a more promising one, the magneto-hydrodynamic (MHD) system, in which the energy of combustion produces a very high velocity jet of hot combustion gases. These pass between the poles of a powerful magnet and, if they are reasonably good conductors, act in the same way as the copper windings of a generator (dynamo) and produce electricity. The energy comes from the kinetic energy of the gases, which are slowed down.

This system has the advantage of doing away with the temperature limitations caused by the need to pass heat through boiler tubes or to have highly stressed metal turbine blades, so the theoretical efficiency can be very high indeed. However, in practice the high gas velocity can only be obtained by dropping the gas temperature considerably below the peak value at the end of combustion and this lowering of gas temperature means that, even when the gas is seeded with potassium, it is still difficult to make it a good conductor. If the fuel is burned with pure oxygen, then the temperatures are high enough, but this is too expensive for an ordinary power station. The simplest practical solution is to raise the combustion temperature by preheating the air to a temperature hotter than the preheat in an open hearth steel-melting furnace, but this will need a new type of refractory preheater to be developed for this use.

A Russian power station of 25 MW fired with natural gas is being operated along these lines, and experimental units have been built in the United States. Designs for a full-sized pulverized coal station have also been developed in the USA. It is probable that pulverized coal-fired central power stations of very high efficiency will still be used as the alternative to nuclear fission at the end of the century. If so, these will be likely to be along the lines of a more sophisticated combined MHD and steam cycle, giving an overall efficiency of 70 per cent, so that less than 60 per cent as much fuel will be needed to give the same amount of electricity as now and the thermal pollution by waste heat will be a quarter as much for a given power. Such a cycle may be obtained by separating the combustion gases having the optimum thermodynamic temperature from thin layers or striations of much hotter gas carrying the seed material and acting as the electrical conductor.

Nuclear fission might produce electricity in the year 2000 by a system having much lower capital cost than the present methods. The largest part (two thirds) of the cost of nuclear electricity is the capital cost of the power station itself. A possible alternative system is the following.

A large sphere is lined with boiler tubes and contains inside it a homogeneous gas consisting of a vapour of a uranium salt at such a high pressure that it forms a critical self-sustaining reactor heating itself to some 5000°K. A convergent divergent nozzle allows the gases to escape at a controlled rate, accelerate to a velocity of a few thousand metres per second while cooling to 2500°K, at which temperature they are still hot enough to be good electrical conductors, producing electricity as they are stopped in a magnetic field. After this they are cooled right down in a boiler, a certain amount of spent reagent is bled off and enough fresh reagent to maintain the cycle is fed in. The gases are then recompressed back to the reactor pressure and returned to the reactor. The whole cycle is built inside a permanent shield and only the electricity made by the MHD generator and the steam cycle and the small bleed and recharge gas flows traverse the wall.

Another exciting possibility is that the large central power station will be completely unnecessary because fully automatic, high-efficiency, small generating units which run without attention for a month or more may have become practicable. If a successful hydrocarbon/air fuel cell has been made, we might even see every house generating its own electricity in one plant combined with the central heating and air conditioning, run on natural gas or oil. (This would be an alternative to the community system envisaged in chapter 5.)

A high-temperature fuel cell is already available which can heat in this way and the temperatures are no higher than those we are already used to in the flames of boilers.

Alternatively again, a 500 kw unit with an improved diesel engine or Stirling cycle engine and generator could be developed with high efficiency (up to 50 per cent overall), very complete combustion and high efficiency silencing. This need not even necessarily have a crank-shaft as a free piston linear AC generator, in which the reciprocation of a pair of balanced opposed pistons moved cotton-reel shaped magnetic cores inside hollow coils, could give a very compact unit.

The principal advantage of such systems would be that they would be independent of the costly and easily disordered mains network. On the other hand, the use of coal or nuclear fission as fuels favours central power stations, so that the most likely future power-production system will probably lie in the finding of some compromise, especially as there will be competition for the limited oil resources. Transmission systems, however, are likely to be mainly underground by the end of the century, as we are sure to have found out by that time how to produce superconductors which can carry the tremendous currents at reasonable voltages. This might be done by using very low-temperature liquid gases to keep the superconductors cool, or perhaps organic chemists will have produced an organic molecule which is superconducting at something like room temperature.

There are two new fuels which will certainly be available by the year 2000. If, as seems likely, we consume fuel by the end of the century at about six times the present rate, the CO_2 (carbon dioxide) could begin to rise fast enough to produce major changes in the world's climate. This is because the decomposition of CO_2 to free oxygen, which takes place in green vegetation, is not nearly fast enough over the whole world's surface to maintain the oxygen content of the atmosphere. Thus, we shall have to produce means of irrigating the deserts to increase the vegetation and probably, eventually, we shall grow some kind of crop-producing food or fodder as well as com-bustible woody matter, such as sugar-cane. In this way the solar energy could be collected over such a large area that our fuel requirements can be produced continuously in spite of the very low collection efficiency (only about 1 per cent of the solar energy falling on the ground is available as fuel for the thermal power station). This would give a truly permanent system, since the CO_2 from the power station could be converted back by the plants to carbon to renew the O_2 in the atmosphere while the H_2O in the power station gases would be either condensed directly out of the gases before they leave the stack to produce fresh water for irrigation, or would form clouds to give rainfall.

Solar energy could also be used as heat or to produce electricity. Direct production of electricity as a result of solar photons falling on a photo-electric surface has already proved practicable and is being used to recharge batteries in satellites, the photocells being on so-called 'sails'. At present this is far too expensive to put over an area of several square kilometres, but an automatic way of producing the surfaces with strips connected in series to give the necessary voltage will probably be produced and may well be used in regions with high sunshine.

No one has so far thought of any means of storing electricity in large quantities, that is to say any electrical equivalent to the gas-holder, but it would be necessary to do so with a solar energy system; as it would be, too, with tidal power generation. The best method known at present is to use the electricity to decompose water and store the oxygen and hydrogen for later recombination in a fuel cell.

The use of solar heat would also need some means of focusing or concentrating, otherwise the heat lost by radiation and convection from the heating surface would prevent the achievement of an adequate temperature to make steam. An ingenious system has been developed in Israel to produce ten horse-power energy: a one-metre diameter cylinder of transparent plastic is blown up by air pressure and has a boiler tube of low boiling point liquid along the axis. The cylinder is placed east–west, and the lower half of it is silvered to reflect solar energy, so that a significant concentration in one dimension is obtained when the system is arranged so that the sun's path is in the plane bisecting the silvered half of the cylinder.

The second fuel that is likely to be in use by the end of the century is nuclear fusion. Since nuclei halfway up the periodic table are the most stable, it is possible to obtain energy just as easily by combining the lightest nuclei as it is by splitting the heaviest nuclei. The most promising reaction is to combine tritium (T^3) with deuterium (D^2); both of these are heavy isotopes of hydrogen (H^1). Deuterium occurs to a significant extent in water, but tritium has to be made artificially. Even these two have to be heated to a temperature of hundreds of millions of degrees K before they will react together, and many laboratory experiments have been carried out in the attempt to attain these controlled temperatures by an electric discharge in a 'magnetic bottle' which keeps the low-pressure gas away from the wall. However, no one has yet achieved a positive power output.

These temperatures are produced by uranium fission in the hydrogen bomb, so once again war technology is far ahead of peace. Also, it may take up to twenty years from the time of obtaining successful laboratory control to translate the method into a practical power station.

Mining and other dangerous operations

As I have already mentioned briefly in chapter 1, the word 'telechirics' has been proposed for all machines in which a human being controls a hand or hands at a distance using the natural skill of his own hands, with feedback to him of sensory information from the artificial hands and the region where these are working.

Remote-control hands seen through closed circuit television cameras have already been developed for handling radioactive materials, and the trained skill of the operator in using his hands can be applied to them without difficulty. The same principle could be used for work in all dangerous situations so that a man could do everything from a safe, comfortable place just as well as if he were on the spot in a burning building, at the bottom of the sea, or down a mine.

This would be especially useful in mining, since the main cost at present is that of making the mine safe, ventilated, pumped free of water, illuminated and spacious enough for men to work in it. The only profitable part of mining is the location of the mineral to be mined and the bringing of it to the surface, and if these two tasks were carried out by machines the cost of mining could be cut to a small fraction of its present figure, with the basic advantage that no human being need ever have to face the dangers and discomforts of work underground.

Finely crushed coal and other solid minerals have already been pumped in a slurry with water for distances of many kilometres, and in Germany a soft coal has been excavated hydraulically and carried in a pipe to a power station where it was burned without separating it from the water.

A machine could be developed which could cut its way into a coal seam, crushing the coal in front of it and pumping the crushed coal to the surface in a stream of water. From the surface, it could then be piped into a power station which could be built in a central coal mining area and fed by some twenty of the mole crushing machines. Provided combustion was complete and all SO_2 was taken out of the flue gases, this might provide a completely satisfactory alternative to the nuclear power station, without the dangers attached to radioactive material.

The mining machine would have to be steered by a man on the surface who would receive from it information about the quality of coal at the top, bottom and two sides of the cut. In this way, the man-controller would know immediately if the machine was straying out of the edge of the seam, or when it had struck a fault. Such a machine might be formed in two parts, each cylindrical in shape, the rear part pushing the front part forward while it stayed, itself, jammed in the hole it had cut by means of three curved feet pushed radially outward by rams. The two parts would be connected by three long-stroke hydraulic ram cylinders, to give a powerful forward cutting stroke. These could be made to cut on a curve in any direction by means of the operator controlling the flow differentially to the three rams. When the cutting-head had advanced a full stroke forward, feet on the cutting-head would be forced out to hold the head in the hole, while the feet on the rear body would be drawn in to release it. By reversing the stroke on the three main rams the body would be pulled forward into the head, dragging with it the two concentric flexible tubes, the electric power cable and the control-signal information coaxial cable.

The inner flexible tube would carry the water flow down to the machine and the space between the inner and the outer tube would carry the coal/water slurry up to the surface. A large submerged electric motor would run the rotating cutting-head and a hydraulic pump to power the movements. The mole-miner would cut radially away from a shaft for a kilometre and then walk itself back to the shaft where it would be hauled to the surface for maintenance. When it had been checked, it would be dropped down the shaft to start a new cut alongside the first one.

Only about 50 per cent of the coal would be extracted, so there would be hardly any subsidence at the surface. Extraction would be from a series of parallel round holes, rather like the original bore and pillar coal mining scheme.

When the mining was for valuable metal ores, especially those that occur only in thin seams, the mole-miner could cut through the ordinary rock and have a spectroscopic detector that would send the operator a continuous series of analyses of all the elements met with during the operation. When the desired ore was signalled in significant quantities, it would be able to rotate its cutting-head to cut all round the front of the hole to find the direction of the vein. The machine could then be operated to follow the vein, testing its dimensions in the manner already described.

In the case of precious metals, such as gold or diamonds, which were scattered in a large body of rock, the mole-miner could cut a hole much larger than it needed for its own progress and eventual return to the surface. Practically all the rock that it cut would be deposited in the hole, but only after it had been through the body of the mole and had the concentrate containing the material separated out. Only this small concentrate would be passed to the surface in the water stream.

Coal used underground

Another way of using coal might also be developed to save the labour of bringing it up above ground-level. The coal could be burnt in its seam with air passed down a flexible tube, allowing electricity and the combustion products to come to the surface. Coal has already been burned underground, with air, to make low-grade producer gas just good enough to be used in a boiler at the pithead. This has been tried in Russia, in the United States and in Britain, although British experiments along these lines have been abandoned because it was thought that too much gas was being lost through the surrounding rock, which was full of fissures left after near-by conventional mining. In this case, such fissures represented a major obstacle since the gas was being carried to the surface by way of a long hole in the coal seam and a vertical shaft.

Future machines for burning coal underground would have to work on a different principle. A possible machine of this type could be shaped like a long cylinder with a diameter equal to the thickness of the coal seam. Its outer casing might be formed of flexible high-temperature resistant plastic which would roll slowly back along the outside and be fed forward inside: in other words, an endless annular belt forming a continuous crawling mechanism that would drive the machine forward through the coal into the hole it would have burnt in the small combustion region at the front of it. This combustion region would contain high-pressure combustion gases.

The inside of such a machine would contain an air compressor and an electricity generator, both driven by a gas-turbine. The air coming down from the surface through a flexible tube would be compressed to ten atmospheres and projected in a high-velocity jet onto the coal face in the sealed region at the front of the machine where it burned the coal. The combustion gases would escape through the gas-turbine, where they would fall back to atmospheric pressure and return to the surface through the hole carrying the air tube. The gas-turbine would drive the air compressor and the electric generator.

Another field where remote-control machines could give enormous benefit to mankind would be in searching for oil. At present the only way to find out whether a dome (which has been shown to exist by the reflection of explosion shocks) carries oil, gas or just water, is to drill a large hole with a 'bit' consisting of a series of thirty-metre long, twenty-centimetre diameter steel tubes screwed together with a cutting-head at the end rotated from a motor on the surface. Every time this bit wears out, it is necessary to unscrew every tube as each one is hauled to the surface, so that it may take weeks to drill one hole even though it may need many holes to be drilled before a fruitful dome is found.

A remote-control drill could be developed, however, which could be steered like the mole-miner, except that the machine could be set to keep an exactly vertical direction, or at any small angle to the vertical. This drill could walk itself quickly to the surface inside a hole lined by a steel strip twenty cm wide. The steel strip would unroll from a large drum to form a helical lining drawn in by the drill and rotated by its screwing action. The drill-head, which would bore a hole of eight to ten cm in diameter, would provide its own drilling pressure by being made in two parts – the lower part being screwed in the cutting direction or rammed a stroke length of one metre, while the upper part jammed in the hole to hold the screw or ram steady.

Remote-controlled machines to work at the bottom of the sea have already been invented, but these could be developed to a point where it would be unnecessary for any human being to go below the surface. A machine could be designed to work at any depth, transmitting all the necessary information to a controller sitting on the surface. The machine would transmit its information by means of tactile sensors, sonar (scanning with a beam of mechanical vibrations in the water) and closed-circuit television through a camera carrying its own light-beam. The machine would probably have two hands and arms, controlled directly by the movements of the human operator's hands and arms, but capable of lifting several tons in weight. It could be powered by electricity carried through a cable, either from land or from a control ship, but it would have enough storage battery power within its own casing to free itself from obstructions and surface automatically if its cable was cut.

Such a machine could be made mobile by having four paddles, each in the form of a wheel with four blades shaped as 60° segments of a flat circle. These blades would be automatically feathered by the rotation of the wheel so that at the lowest position they would be parallel to the axis and, at the highest position, in plane with the wheel disc. The machine could therefore 'swim' by rotating its four paddles at a high speed or, at a slower speed, roll along in the sand at the sea-bottom.

Another dangerous job that could be carried out by telechiric machines is the dousing of oil-well fires. These fires usually occur when a drill strikes a high-pressure gas source and ignites it to give an extremely hot flame. The present method of extinguishing these flames is to build a crude passageway of corrugated-iron sheets to protect a trained fireman while he runs up as close as possible to the flame and throws an explosive charge into it. If he is lucky, the explosion then extinguishes the flame and he is left to deal with only a cold jet of gas. If he is unlucky, the situation becomes extremely dangerous for him.

There is no need for people to face such danger. A device like a small army tank could be made to be controlled by a man at a safe distance from the fire. This tank, shielded to stand the full heat of the fire, could be driven up to the flame, where it would put a heavy concrete plug with an open tube and valve over the top of the well-hole. It would hold this plug down firmly, ram it in and close the valve. The flame would be extinguished and the tank could retreat again.

We have already developed, in my laboratory, a prototype remote-control fire-fighting machine. The machine is steered and driven through its front wheel and tours a building round a track marked out by a heavy black line which the machine senses by photocells. It has a

97

gyro-compass to check its orientation and it checks distance by counting the revolutions of the driving wheel. The driving wheel carries a photocell in a stalk and as the machine 'hunts', following the path, the photocell scans an arc in front of it. If it sees a bright light from a fire, it leaves the track and homes on the light. An arm carrying a switch swings forward, the heat of the fire closes the switch which stops the forward movement of the machine and brings two fire-extinguishers into operation, extinguishing the fire.

This machine might be equally useful for putting out fires in homes and could be made part of community fire-fighting equipment – but I shall talk about machines for the home in the next chapter.

9

The home and the community in a Creative Society

'It is in the individual home,' I have written in chapter 5, 'that the greatest diversity would be found in a way of life that had as its whole objective the encouragement of people to think for themselves, and to be themselves and to create with their hands.'

However, certain basic common needs would have to be met in any living-unit acceptable in a prosperous, high-technology state: full insulation against the prevailing weather conditions; insulation against noise, smells, dirt, insects and so on; security against unwanted entry, which must include all possibility of 'bugging' devices or any other means of monitoring and restriction on freedom of speech and action; protection against fire; a fully-controllable heating system; washing facilities; power for light, cooking and communications systems; adequate arrangements for sewage and rubbish disposal; privacy; access for both pedestrians and delivery of goods; and, above all, space in which to live and work without a feeling of frustration and restriction. Space, particularly, I believe, to carry on a hobby that has nothing to do with the individual's normal work in earning a living.

My own craft hobby is wood-carving. I find it enormously therapeutic and relaxing, especially after a distressing committee meeting which has left me feeling 'if only I had said so and so' and 'is it all worth while?' It means so much to me, in fact, that I have developed two portable sets of tools, one for the boot of my car so that I can make things when I am on holiday, and a second set I can carry in a camera case and use in foreign hotels. I am also an inveterate do-it-yourselfer, feeling my house was not my home until I had made it, with my own hands, the place in which my wife and I wanted to live. There would have to be scope, in a Creative Society, for making a home exactly what its owners, temporary or permanent, wanted it to be. There are already building systems which allow for walls and partitions to be easily moved, and spray-on paint could change colour schemes within an hour or so. There would also need to be space, in a Creative Society, for every home to have its own workshop and the chance to arrange certain windows to give the right light for a studio.

Not everyone would want to relax with painting or a craft hobby, of course. Some people would obviously get more pleasure out of reading or playing a musical instrument or writing poetry than from carving wood, but the chance to create with our hands, in some part of our daily lives, does satisfy some particularly basic need in human beings. We are said, after all, to have three kinds of 'brain' or intelligence: intelligence with abstract ideas, mechanical intelligence and emotional or social intelligence. If any one of these three 'brains' is not adequately exercised, it will fail to develop that part of our personalities, and we shall have less well-being in consequence. Craft-work is trebly valuable in combining all three forms of intelligence, and might of itself therefore, if actively encouraged, cure many social ills. The great advantage of work done as a hobby, too, rather than to earn a living, is that it can be done without any time limit and to the degree of perfection that satisfies the individual. The slow, meticulous worker can feel as great a satisfaction as the impatient, 'dashing' innovator. Everyone is 'right', and we all need to find the comfort and reassurance of 'rightness' in our private lives if we are to give society our tough, fighting best.

This would apply to women as much as to men, in a Creative Society. The 'little woman', the 'lady', the protected woman is already a lost concept to the new generation, but the fact will remain that girls will always be less physically strong than boys and more vulnerable emotionally, especially when they are assailed by any stage of the procreative process. Although biologists seem to be working on some very peculiar frozen supermarket select-your-father processes that seem unlikely to satisfy any final female emotional need, nobody has yet invented a way for anyone not a woman to have her own baby. However, professional women, even today, can take a very minimal time off to have their children, and with both sexes educated together and trained to all the jobs that would remain necessary even in a Creative Society, with video-phone links enabling shopping and perhaps even a young mother's office-work to be done at home; with older relatives and with many friends, members of the same community; with part-time nursery services available; with husbands working shorter hours, no young mother would be left in the sort of restricted isolation to which suburban living so often condemns women today. Nor would a couple who had met at university or while they were working together on some later project where they had enjoyed each other's company up to twenty-four hours a day, be left to feel that starting a family had broken up this unity and forced them into leading almost separate lives, perhaps never to be so successfully linked again.

Both partners in a marriage in the Creative Society might well work at least some part of their time from their home, helped by the video-phone, the information services available by video-phone link, and such inventions as the dictation-typewriter, which I have already described. Even the vexed question of who should be responsible for the household chores could be settled by the use of robot domestic help.

Robot home-help

Automatic food-mixers, washing-machines and dish-washers are already available, of course, but a domestic robot could be produced which tidied, dusted, laid the table for meals, made beds, scrubbed, vacuum-cleaned, polished, scoured saucepans, baths and ovens, put itself away in a cupboard when it had finished and plugged itself into the mains to recharge its power-source batteries.

Plate 6 is a model of the possible form such a domestic robot might take. It does not look like a human being in any way because it would be designed to use continuous rotation in its joints in place of the reciprocation of human joints; it would use structural members of metal with a much higher strength to weight ratio than bone; and its range of activities would be much less varied than those achievable by even the least athletic human being. It would, however, be about the same height as a human being, with a width and length dictated by its need to go through doorways and manœuvre in rooms filled with furniture. It would be able to vary its movements in a pre-instructed way according to variations in the external situation such as an un-expected obstacle which needed to be circumnavigated, picked up, or put on a shelf. It would also detect and modify its movements to dirt spots in certain areas, and to finding objects for which it was searching in unexpected places.

The base would be a four-wheel drive-carriage, the wheels having twelve sprung spokes but no rim, so that they could carry the robot up a flight of stairs designed for human legs. The upper surface of the base-carriage would be a tray for carrying objects up to dustbin size and with several sockets carrying tools such as a high-speed rotating scourer, a low-speed, high-torque rotating device for screwing and unscrewing, a vacuum-cleaner nozzle, and water and air jet nozzles for soaps and powders. All these tools would carry their own specialized motors and could be picked up in the robot's 'hand', remaining connected to the batteries in the base by flexible cable which would unwind from a spring rewind drum.

Incidentally, one of these handtools would be useful, even today, as a household tool and could be produced as the housewife's equivalent of a handyman's electric drill. This would be an electrically driven universal scrubber, scourer and polisher, which would run off a motor on wheels with a flexible power shaft which could be held in the hand against the surface to be treated, or clamped on a stand by the sink so that a pan to be scoured could be held against it with both hands. The working head would consist of either a pair of brushes, reciprocating in opposition with a stroke varying from a few millimetres to ten centimetres and frequency varying inversely, or of two concentric circular brushes rotating in opposite directions to balance the torque. The brushes could be changeable to wire, nylon or polisher, and soap grits and polishes could be fed in at a low rate automatically.

This could be done with the robot, also. The robot's hand would be supported on an arm with the 'shoulder' at the top of a rigid pillar $1\frac{1}{2}$ m above the ground. The two parts of the arm would each be 1 m long so that the arm could fold up against the pillar or reach a hand 2 m horizontally in any direction from the shoulder. It could also reach the ground at any point around the carriage or reach up to $2\frac{1}{2}$ m vertically above the ground. The hand could be rotated continuously about three space axes on the end of the arm, its parallel jaws opening up to 30 cm, but having special 'V' grooves to hold cylindrical or conical objects of any diameter pointing forward or sideways. One of the jaws would be sprung to hold wedge-shaped or conical objects firmly. Thus, by careful design, the hand could grasp as wide a range of shapes and a larger range of sizes than a human hand, but using only one controlled grasping movement in place of the twenty that five human digits can perform (four for each digit, by way of one sideways and three joints bending forwards.) However, the robot would not be able to hold several objects at once, nor would it be able to juggle!

It would have a second hand, with three fingers sticking up from the base, so that the mobile hand could pick up an object, such as a saucepan, and place it in this second hand, which would rotate slowly about a vertical axis while the mobile hand cleaned it with a scouring tool.

The robot would be equipped with a scanning range-finder device, operated by either light or sound, fixed above its 'shoulder' and with a spring-wire antenna for detecting obstacles in front of the carriage. It would probably also have a tiny television camera fixed to its hand so that it would 'look at' objects and decide into which one of a limited set of categories they must be allocated by the pattern recognition device in its computer-brain in order to take appropriate action, such as dividing crockery from cutlery.

Every family in a Creative Society would be able to afford a domestic robot, hiring it rather than buying it, so that it could be serviced at regular monthly intervals or at times of breakdown. It would, however, be individual to one particular household, since it would have to be programmed, initially, for the particular family's needs. For instance, it could be trained to understand the layout of the home by steering it, the first time, under hand-control while it 'learned its way around'. By this method it could be instructed to return displaced furniture to a 'recognized' position – or, equally, to leave the furniture in a new position. It could be taught positions for articles on shelves or in cupboards, and if these were on the floor could pick them up and put them away in their right places. It could be taught a routine of house-cleaning, dialled by the householder as a code. A safety device would be built in so that the user would only need to shout 'stop' for all the robot's circuits to be disconnected.

Like all other machines made in the Creative Society, the robot would be built to last at least twenty-five years, instead of being designed for obsolescence, like the present-day domestic equipment. This would save raw materials, manufacturing costs and capital outlay.

I have had a lot of publicity in the press for this domestic robot. The only part of it in prototype in my laboratory, built to demonstrate the practicability of making such a machine with present-day technology, is a robot table-clearing device. This has one 'sight' and two touch – a soft and a strong touch – pressure sensors. It locates an object at any point along the length of a table by moving along the side of the table until the object casts a shadow into its photo-electric 'eye'. This triggers the hand, which moves across the table until it touches the object. The hand then grasps the object – whatever its size – by closing until a strong pressure on the pressure sensor in the hand indicates that it has a firm grip. The hand then lifts the object off the table, the arm brings the hand and object back onto a circular tray on the base of the robot, and the tray rotates and clears the object away, leaving room for the next object to be placed on the tray as the robot continues its advance along the side of the table.

The principles involved in this machine have been used in other, more fundamentally useful, inventions of mine, but the gimmick of a robot 'char' has caught the imagination of our present 'affluent society', with its obsession with gimmicks and this, to me, has been the project's greatest worth – it has brought me the chance to talk about other inventions of mine that I feel are more important, the machines I shall describe in the next chapter.

The home in the community

The ideal of a home is that it is a sanctuary, a private place of safety to retreat to for food and sleep and being yourself and doing whatever you want to do. In a society geared to give every member a chance to find self-fulfilment and as much companionship as they want, with space in the home and comfort and facilities for craftwork and similar activities, there would be a good chance that many more homes would provide this ideal. Human happiness, however, would still, finally, depend on human relationships, so that the community would need to have available individual houses for rent by the 'single' of any age. The essential here, however, would be that such accommodation should not be set apart from houses owned by families so that all age-groups and people in different stages of emotional stress or development could live near each other and help each other.

It would also be necessary, as I have said, for each community to organize facilities, available by a world-wide standard procedure, for renting houses and furniture to people arriving from other places, and of integrating such people into the life of the community as quickly as possible, to the extent of knowing where to go for basic necessities or to involving themselves in the social life and giving of services to the community, as they wished.

Trolley-seats would, of course, be available for immediate hire for luggage, and the shuttle service I have already described would bring goods to the home and dispose of rubbish. Since the present-day United States housewife, driving a big car, uses a great deal of fuel, the world resources saved by this more economical method of transport and shopping would, on its own, be considerable.

If we continue our present way of life, a world citizen, by the year 2000, will consume nine tons of coal equivalent a year, whereas every necessity for a satisfactory life – good food and clothes, foreign travel, local mobility and warm houses – can certainly be produced at two to three tons of coal equivalent per head which is the present world average, and therefore natural resources could be conserved.

Natural resources could also be conserved if goods were produced only if they met people's genuine needs. At the moment, modern marketing theory recognizes two types of innovation – the first is the development of ideas simply because somebody has thought of them, regardless of whether these ideas satisfy a need or not; the second type of innovation starts with the identification of a need in society regardless of whether the technology is immediately available to serve that need. The second kind of innovation is therefore directed towards the achievement of a defined objective: 'I have discovered this problem, how can I solve it?', rather than 'I have thought of this object, what can I do with it?'

Progressive marketing men are beginning to find that the second type of innovation is not only less wasteful but, in meeting the real needs of the ordinary man, may even be more profitable.

But there is a long way to go. What the more far-sighted see as truth today may take years to win a big enough public acceptance to make it normal practice – but I shall talk about this in chapter 11.

10

Social responsibility in a Creative Society

With plenty of leisure time for everyone, and a sense of responsibility towards others a recognized and honoured ideal in the Creative Society, care of the physically and mentally sick, and of the elderly, might probably be left, to some extent, to voluntary helpers. In time, too, in a society without excessive aggression, pollution, frustration or fast cars, there might come to be a lot less mental and physical illness and people might live to be well over one hundred before they would count as being 'elderly' at all. The understanding of medicine, too, might become so widespread that people could usually be nursed in their own homes and only rarely have to go into hospital.

However, until such a point was reached, no amount of solicitude or goodwill would finally substitute for trained professional skill, and although a sense of vocation would receive every encouragement in a society that would both pay well and honour its healers, doctors and nurses, like everyone else, would be greatly helped if the drudgery and routine could be done for them by machines.

In this particular area, in fact, work has already been started – although at a comparatively slow rate because, while we are willing to spend enormous sums and scientific skill on the development of war weapons, there is very little money available for healing devices. However, applied physics has produced a number of measuring instruments which have helped doctors to diagnose their patients' ailments. The first of these was the X-ray which, of course, enabled doctors to examine their patients internally without surgery. Another invention was the electro-encephalograph, which records the fluctuations of small electric voltages corresponding to the activity in the brain, and a further development was the electrocardiogram, which does the same thing for the physical action of the heart.

A recent invention has been the radio pill, which emits detectable radio signals giving a measurable indication of temperature, pressure or acidity, as it passes through the digestive system. Work is now in progress, too, on a means of scanning the whole skin temperature of a patient by infra-red emission so that regions which are abnormally hot or cold, by a degree or two, can be detected.

By the year 2000 these diagnostic instruments should have been taken to the point where a doctor can seat his patient in a chair where a machine can scan his or her whole body, internally and externally, and give an immediate indication of any abnormality. This would be detected by physical quantities such as density, temperature, pressure tension and electrical pulsation, and the results of the scan would be compared on a computer with normality and with previous scans on the same patient. The computer would then print out a diagram of the body, showing all the relevant data. If the doctor suspected a certain ailment or wanted more details about a particular part of the body, he could scale up the probing devices and instruct the computer to give this further information. The basic principle of the mechanism for this machine might be xerography – that is to say, the use of two pencil beams of radio waves of less than one millimetre wavelengths such that their point of intersection could be made at any place in the body, the interaction of the beams giving a scattered radiation which could be measured in various directions. By chopping the beams and varying the frequency, signals could be obtained which were differentially related to the physical properties of the scattering point.

The use of such machines would not reduce the need for doctors but would relieve the doctor of much guesswork by allowing him to see what was wrong at any point inside his patient. This would enable him to play his role as a physical counsellor; to distinguish with certainty between real and imaginary ailments; and to ensure that his patients' enjoyment of life was harmed as little as possible by physiological factors.

New tools, too, will probably be invented, since although engineers have already produced many beautifully designed tools for surgeons, they still basically use hand-power for cutting, sewing, tying knots, chiselling and sawing. However, recently laser beams have been used for welding eye retinas in place, and in Russia a stapler has been produced that joins two severed arteries together by means of tantalum staples, after the ends have been cuffed over.

Generally, however, the surgeon hand-sews arteries together by half-circular needles and fine thread, down to one millimetre diameter. Experiments are therefore being carried out in my laboratory to develop an automatic lock-stitcher which would put in five double-loop stitches simultaneously. We hope eventually to make this lock-stitcher in even smaller sizes than one millimetre, and a successful sewing-machine of this type would enable severed fingers and limbs to be reattached, because all the necessary arteries, and even nerve sheaths, could be rapidly sewn together.

A surgical operation in the year 2000

This is my pre-vision of a surgical operation performed at the end of the century:

The patient lies on the cushioned floor of a large box with glass sides. He has a breathing and anaesthetic mask on his nose and mouth. Beside him are rows of trays carrying all the tools the surgeon might need to use, each tool's handle being in the form of two hollow cylindrical tubes. These tools – scissors, forceps, sewing devices previously loaded with thread, chisels, saws and welding devices – are all electrically operated, the relative movement of the two parts of the handle controlling their manipulation.

A further sterilized tray of tools stands ready to replace the first set through a sterile lock. The whole box in which the patient lies is sterilized between operations both by steam and ultra-violet rays. The roof of the box carries a television camera with a lens that can be moved by the surgeon anywhere over the patient. It can also be controlled to give a two-, four- or ten-fold magnification on a series of television screens outside.

The box-lid also carries eight pairs of arms, each ending in two rods which can fit into any of the tools. The surgeon sits at a control-desk with four pairs of loops in front of him hanging from overhead telescopic rods, and with a television screen facing him. His assistant sits at another desk with a television screen and another four pairs of loops. The loops are suspended in such a way that as the operator puts his four left-hand fingers into one loop and his left-hand thumb into the other of a pair, he can move the two loops about with his hand freely in all three dimensions, and he can open and close the two loops. These loops are connected to one arm inside the box by an electric or hydraulic control system, and in such a way that the two toolholding rods exactly reproduce any movement the surgeon makes outside, including all three rotations in space as well as the three displacements.

Using a pair of arms, the surgeon can pick up a pair of tools and watch the remote operation as closely as if he were bending over the patient, moving the television camera about inside the operating box by a control worked by movements of his head. He can use his tools with as much freedom as he could use them if they were directly in his hands, but the control system gives him a steadiness of hand far greater than that which he could achieve without machine aid. Not only do the toolholders follow his hand movements exactly, but he can feel the resistance to movement and the weight of the tools, just as he would if he were handling them. When he wishes to hold some part with clamps or forceps, he can place these in position with one toolholder, lock this in place by removing his hand from the control loops, and use another toolholder with his other hand. Moreover, the steel rods holding the tools are much less bulky than his fingers, so that access to limited spaces is greatly increased.

It is even possible for one pair of rods to be one quarter the diameter and length of the others and to reproduce the movement of the surgeon's hands on a quarter scale. When the surgeon uses this pair of tools, the television screens magnify the image four times so that he sees and feels all the tool movements as though they were full size and the patient was four times his actual size.

Machines to help nurses

At present, much of a nurse's time and energy is spent doing all sorts of non-nursing jobs, but in a Creative Society engineers would be encouraged to develop machines which would relieve nurses of all these chores so that they could devote their time and energy to true nursing, which involves a sympathetic understanding of people's emotions as well as of their ailments. All routine checking and form-filling could be done by instruments plugged in to a central recorder, which could also be instructed by the doctors about the treatment necessary for each patient.

Conveyor-belt systems could carry food rapidly from the kitchens to the patients, with electrical hot-plates to prevent the food getting cold on the way.

Bedpans could be plumbed in on a flexible system, and all cleaning of floors and walls could be carried out automatically.

Many ingenious hospital beds have already been designed, including those which overcome the tendency of the sitting-up patient to slide down the bed. This has mostly been done by hinging the bed at a line under the base of the spine and again under the knee so that the thigh-support can be inclined downwards towards the head when the back and calves are inclined the other way.

In a Creative Society, the present argument that developing a perfectly designed hospital bed is not a good enough commercial proposition would, of course, be seen as nonsense and a bed would be developed which could be adjusted to be comfortable in any position from that of an upright chair to a head-down tilt of 20°. Such a bed would also be made available to every patient in every community hospital in the world.

One activity which is extremely awkward for nurses and hospital porters today is the task of lifting an inert patient in order to change his sheets or to put him on a trolley to take him to the operating theatre. In my laboratory, we are developing a wedge, with belts on the two faces which move backwards at exactly the same speed at which the wedge is pushed forward, so that the patient can be lifted onto the wedge with practically zero friction. By mounting this device onto a powered trolley, the patient can be lifted off the bed without any muscular effort on the part of the nurse.

The intensive care units of hospitals are, in fact, already becoming mechanized in that instant warning is given if the condition of any patient changes for the worse. Another development is in breathing aids which amplify the faintest breath of a patient to ensure that enough oxygen reaches his lungs. Extension of this sort of development could soon ensure that nobody died who might possibly be restored to health, but how far doctors will feel it is right to 'strive officiously to keep alive' a body whose brain has been hopelessly damaged by illness or accident will surely always be a matter of individual conscience, based on a deep concern to prevent pointless suffering, of the living family or dependants as well as of the half-dead individual himself.

Physiotherapy, massage and manipulation already use a combination of manual dexterity, based on real knowledge of the body's needs, with help from various simple mechanical devices such as weights and pulleys for traction. More sophisticated machines will certainly be developed, but these treatments will probably be still largely carried out by hand because they represent a human service which needs an element of sympathy that will never be conveyed by a machine.

Artificial limbs and organs

Plastic valves with ping-pong balls to replace the beautifully stream-lined flexible tricuspid valve of the heart have been successfully installed in people's bodies, and the cardiac pacemaker is used fairly frequently. This device is implanted into the body to give an electric pulse to the heart to stimulate its regular action when the natural nervous impulse is weak. It contains a tiny mercury battery, and an electronic circuit is connected to a point in the heart by a fine wire. The batteries last about two years, after which an operation is necessary to replace the unit, because electric leads, for recharging, cannot be run through the skin.

A radioactive powered battery with a very much longer life has been tested in a dog. This experiment was carried out in the United States. Very recently, too, a mechanical pump has been tested in animals which circulates the blood handled by the heart's left ventricle and so eases the load on the heart. This requires much more power than the pacemaker, and nickel cadmium batteries are implanted which can be recharged by electricity carried electromagnetically from a plate placed outside the chest to one implanted inside. These are in a very early stage of development as the batteries only operate the pump for three quarters of an hour, but take one and a half hours to recharge. However, they do point the way to an entirely artificial heart, which can be controlled by the patient's nerve system and operated by artificial muscles powered from the chemical reaction of food and oxygen carried by the bloodstream, in the same way as a natural heart. When this is ready to be used, it will no longer be necessary to take a heart from a corpse to replace that of a live man – although, of course, the same difficulties will have to be overcome of nullifying the body's natural rejection mechanism.

In the United States, a device has been used successfully to save the lives of several patients whose hearts are temporarily working too weakly to keep them alive. A rubber bulb is inserted by way of an artery into the aorta and the feeble heartbeats are used as signals to control an external pump which causes the bulb to expand and contract in synchronism with the heart, and thus to produce a more powerful pumping action while the heart recovers.

In 1969, for the first time, a small engine was operated which, like a muscle, can convert chemical energy directly to mechanical energy without the need to go through the stage of converting the energy to heat. The electric battery, of course, converts chemical energy to electrical energy, and the steam engine and internal combustion engine convert energy by means of heat (losing most of the energy in the process). This new engine, however, uses a special fibre thread wound round two tapered pulleys which it drives as a result of its powerful contraction when it enters a strong salt solution. The contraction is reversed after it leaves the salt solution and enters a vessel containing pure water. The energy comes from the gradual mixing of the salt into the pure water.

This is still a long step from a mechanical muscle as compact and powerful as an animal muscle fed by a bloodstream carrying chemicals and controlled by minute electrical signals carried by nerves. The nearest mechanical 'artificial muscle' at the moment is an elastic tube developed in Japan with longitudinal inextensible threads, so that, when compressed air or pressurized water is fed into it, it can bulge out and draw its ends together with a powerful force.

However, artificial muscles will probably be constructed within the foreseeable future, not only to replace damaged natural muscles, but also for manipulating artificial arms and legs. It is already possible, in fact, to connect electrodes onto the skin at each end of a sound muscle and for these electrodes to pick up a signal proportional to the contraction of the muscle. The signal comes from the nerve's electrical impulse to the muscle, and we might eventually be able to connect directly to such nerves, although the area of contact would be so small that the current to be amplified might not be sufficient – and, again, as with the artificial heart, the problem of the body's rejection-mechanism would have to be overcome.

The electrode control system, however, is especially useful for artificial hands and arms, because the person who has had these amputations can learn to use such a mechanism with great skill. At present the controls are powered by compressed gas cylinders or electric batteries, and it is not possible to have a powered artificial leg because all our mechanical methods of carrying power, except the internal combustion engine, are much too heavy.

A fuel cell operating on air and a special liquid fuel such as methyl alcohol could probably be developed to drive an artificial leg electrically, but the electric motors or linear actuators would, once more, be heavy. The internal combustion engine would probably always be too noisy and smelly, so we can conclude that the powered artificial leg, when it is finally produced, will have its artificial muscles reacting their own chemical fuel (perhaps methyl alcohol) with air to produce muscular contractions directly.

The method of control of the knee movement presents the greatest problem. Non-powered artificial legs, operated by the stump of the thigh, at the moment either have a knee which is permanently rigid during walking, or else one which can be locked rigid by throwing it forward so that a catch must be released to bend it.

My laboratory has constructed an electrically operated pair of legs which bend the knee in relation to the thigh movement in the same cycle as a human pair of legs, but these studies show that for stepping up or over an obstacle the cycle must be varied, so that the walker must have easily operated control of each step. Perhaps the first powered knee will be worked automatically from the swinging of the thigh and therefore only be suitable for walking on level ground, but control mio-electrically by the contraction of the arm muscles might become feasible, so that a legless person could learn to walk quite normally by swinging his arms, or a person paralysed below the waist by a spinal lesion could control his leg muscles, again by swinging his arms.

Heart-lung machines that pump and oxygenate the blood during an operation are already in use, and so, of course, are artificial kidney machines. In both cases the human body does its task with less power and in a very small fraction of the volume of the machine. This is because the chemical engineering of constructing semipermeable boundaries and packing a large area into a very small space (with the two fluids kept separate) and the mechanical engineering of non-turbulent flow pumps and valves (from controlled flexible parts operated by their own muscular tissue) are both branches of engineering in which the natural growth of the body is far better than anything we can so far manufacture.

People who have no kidneys can be kept alive by regular visits to a large and expensive kidney machine, through which their blood circulates while the impurities in it are extracted through the semipermeable membrane. They have to have an artery cut and 'quills' inserted to allow the blood to leave the body every time they are connected to the machine. Work is already being done to try to develop an artificial kidney small enough to be carried by the patient, but this involves a permanent connection through the skin and it is almost impossible to prevent bacteria entering through such a connection. Thus, a completely artificial kidney will have to be developed, as small as a real kidney so that it can be implanted in its place.

This will be difficult, but the most difficult problem of all may be restoring eyesight to a person whose eyes are useless. The first step, however, has already been taken: this is giving the blind some of their missing information by way of their ears or fingers. A blind person's walking stick has been developed which, when it is pointed at any object, reflects sonar rays and indicates distance from the object by a change of buzzing note in earphones worn by the blind person, the change being proportional to the distance the object is away from the stick.

The next step in helping the blind could be the production of a two-dimensional picture of everything in front of them by means of a sonar or light scanner. Each point would have a physical quantity, which could be felt by the fingers, corresponding to the distance any object was away from the scanner, which could, of course, be turned in all directions. The 'quantity' could take the form of a small electric voltage; an actual physical raising of tiny rods in the surface so that a bas relief was produced; a magnetic field intensity which could be felt by the force on tiny magnets fixed to the finger tips; or even surface temperature variations.

Experiments have also begun on the possibility of communicating to the actual brain messages as complex as those that come from the eye along the optic nerve – which correspond to some millions of points for each of which a light intensity and a colour signal are necessary. These experiments are based on the idea of having a microwave receiver inside the scalp which can transmit electrical pulses to the brain, coupled electromagnetically to a microwave transmitter in a hat, which in turn could get its information from a television camera. To enable a blind person to 'see' with this apparatus, it would be necessary for him or her to learn to piece together a picture from a single rapidly changing impulse from the television scanner, instead of from millions of simultaneous impulses which we have learnt to group into a picture. When it is possible to convert the scanned information into a picture and couple these into the brain cells which give us sight, then an artificial eye will give a blind person full sight again.

Machines to help the elderly and crippled to lead a normal life

We have already made in my laboratory a prototype machine which will carry a seated adult up a flight of stairs. If this principle is applied to a wheelchair, so that the user can change from the normal wheel to a spoked wheel for stair-climbing, a crippled person with sound arms could be greatly helped by being able not only to go upstairs in buildings but also to climb a small set of steps into a van and then drive it away without aid.

We also have in prototype a seat designed for use in a kitchen or workshop, in which the user can sit all the time, and yet move as freely backwards, forwards or sideways as if he were standing on his own legs, merely pushing a switch in the direction he wishes to go and rescuing dropped tools with a stick topped by a mechanical 'hand', which can be worked by a lever at the sitter's end.

Another machine which has been developed by us to a prototype stage is a bannister rail beside an ordinary staircase, the whole height of its rising distance. A person who has any sort of ailment which prevents him making the physical effort of climbing stairs can carry a special walking-stick which fits into the bannister rail, which then moves upward or downward when he presses a switch on the walking-stick. During the time that the user is being transported, he can lean his weight against the horizontal bar formed by the walking-stick so that he does no more work than walking on the level. The stick is raised by a motor-driven chain and the machine can be installed in any building, including private houses.

These examples all typify the way in which the ingenuity of the engineer could help physically handicapped people. It is, however, almost impossible for such machines to become widely available to the people who need them at the present time because, under our present economic system, governments will not give priority to paying for their manufacture and commercial firms cannot produce them at a low enough figure to meet a mass-market price-range. In a Creative

I

Society, it would be a first essential to the healthy to help people who are handicapped to lead as nearly normal a life as possible. In general, people would much rather have aids in their own homes than live in institutions, and this, too, would be arranged as far as possible through community services.

Engineers could soon develop machines which would give people mobility in spite of arthritis, rheumatism and other crippling diseases. They could also develop communications systems so that neighbours or relations could be summoned if a person living alone had an accident; or produce a device by which a doctor or a relative could check by fully automatic video-phone link that all was well with a patient or a member of the family.

Many cases of leg paralysis are due to the nerves in the spine being damaged or severed, and these might eventually be completely curable since it should not be impossible to reconnect nerves or, alternatively, to operate a paralytic's own legs by mio-electric signals from his arms.

One development, again from my own laboratory, which may slow the onset of arthritis considerably, is a pair of hollow legs which can carry a person's weight from a bicycle saddle through to soles under their shoes, so that they can walk without the pain caused by the pressure on the defective bearing joints and thus exercise their muscles and joints without discomfort. Ultimately, we may well find a method of replacing the defective part of a bone and putting in a new lubricating layer which is as effective in carrying the load freely and without pain as the original natural healthy bone structure.

11

What can, and must, be done

Alvin Toffler, in *Future Stock* (Bodley Head, 1970), has suggested what he calls 'collaborative Utopianism' as a means of finding a way to man's physical and psychological survival. I realize that no individual's ideas for Utopia would be likely to be acceptable, in detail, to everyone in the world and that the Utopia I have described in this book – although it is 'collective' to the extent that it is based on the discoveries of many engineers and scientists – does not answer all the questions or solve all the problems.

The way of life I have outlined, however, would offer most individuals the chance to lead a life they found enjoyable, however diverse their individual tastes; and the machines I have described would solve problems of pollution (by both noxious substances and noise), conserve raw materials, eliminate malnutrition, do away with boredom, danger and drudgery in daily work, heal the sick, and enlarge people's horizons through travel, communication and education. It seems to me to be too easy a thing only to make an assessment of our dilemmas. Some of us must find the courage to lead towards a possible way out.

I hope, at least, with this book, my ideals will reach a wider audience than those I have talked to already in the lecture hall: at best, that I may inspire others to develop my ideas in their own fields and return them to me enlarged so that somewhere, sometime – but as soon as possible, because time is short – we can get together and work out practical realities. This is essential. We cannot delay, debating, too long. We are all well aware, now, that what Buckminster Fuller has called 'the design-science revolution' (*Utopia or Oblivion*, Bantam Books, 1969; Allen Lane, 1970), the wider development of the nineteenth-century Industrial Revolution, has become a bolting horse, out of control, and that we are all on its back. We know that we must find a way to grasp the reins and control the steed and make it trot, rather than gallop, in the direction we need it to go. Our difficulty is in choosing the power source for this achievement and the course to ride once control is attained.

I have tried to prove that we do have a power source, technology, and that it can be controlled for good, rather than for evil. We can begin, therefore, right away, to establish our priorities, which does not mean, as some people have suggested, calling a halt to progress, but of accelerating development and innovation in the agreed direction and decelerating development and innovation in less desirable areas.

How we do this is open to debate. People educated in the arts may largely champion the ideals of democratic evolution, like those put forward in *The Greening of America* (Random House, 1970; Allen Lane, 1971), because they are zealous for the freedom of the individual and therefore fear the placement of too much power with any one section of the community. But Charles Reich's climate of 'Consciousness' would need a considerable number of years for its growth, and would take more years still to influence governments, especially the international policies of governments. Before that time we might well have blown ourselves to bits or poisoned our environment beyond repair. So again, I feel I am speaking with the practicality of an engineer when I say we must act positively and at once, to make a start – at any rate, some of us.

We cannot all, everyone in the world, get together and talk. Some people must take the lead, and I would argue that one group of such people must be engineers, technologists and scientists. First, as I have said in chapter 1, my professional colleagues have specialist knowledge of how to go about things as diverse as reorganizing food supplies, finding the causes and cures of pollution, harnessing natural resources, inventing machines that serve needed purposes and so on. Second, we could agree to refuse to invent or make any further weapons, or machines that harm people in any way. Third, we already form an international community for the communication of ideas, meeting each other all over the world and talking with a freedom certainly not available to politicians. We are a community concerned with the truth about the nature of the universe, not with political pressures, one-upmanship or keeping up with the Jones's. We are the people who brought the great advances I have outlined in chapters 2 and 3 to the world and the people who could bring the machines I have talked about in the later chapters into being.

No little part of the discontent in our present age, I am certain, lies in the indignity that labour has become. The craftsman had pride. If there is any pride taken in the repetitive, boring, soul-destroying work in industry today, it lies in the basically sanguine nature of the human beings concerned who, refusing to be robbed of pride and dignity, make a cause for it even in the mean circumstances that are all there is available to them. Humanity deserves something better than meanness. Whatever evil man has committed, he is also capable of doing great good and must be given the opportunity to develop this capability.

Machine slaves would make us all the free citizens, the élite, of a Hellenistic society that might create a golden age of art and craft and philosophy to surpass the fragile brilliance that was Athens four hundred years before Christ, of which the light still shines down the years to us. In this hope, I intend to make it very clear that I am in no way proposing the rule of the world by scientists. If science has produced truths that served mankind in the last two centuries, the arts have produced truths that have saved it. Even in the arts, the *avant-garde* are impeded by the 'what's good enough for my father is good enough for me' and the 'will it pay?' outlooks that stagnate science and invention. The 'two cultures' are fast becoming one, which is made manifest by such things as Buckminster Fuller's geodesic domes and the extension of the British Design Council to include engineering design.

Design, after all, whether it is engineering, architecture or any other type of design, might be described as the application of scientific knowledge, principles and judgment in the creation of products and systems to satisfy human social, economic, ecological and aesthetic needs.

Serving as acolytes to both science and art are a public never before so educated and aware: becoming aware, more and more, that wealth without moral responsibility leads to malaise and unhappiness – in other words the sort of decadence our Victorian grandparents or great-grandparents trumpeted against, and sounded narrow-minded and hysterical as they said it. But the 'affluent society' and the misery it has brought is a demonstration of the wider truth behind the Victorians' too-rigid morality: total self-indulgence, not as a change but as a way of life, leads only to emptiness. We need a balance. We need to give as well as to take. We need definitions.

There are two myths in science: one is that the pursuit of knowledge justifies its own ends, regardless of the consequences and the way in which knowledge is applied; the other is the idea that in certain circumstances of national need the end, such as the finishing of the Second World War, justifies the means, such as the atomic bomb. Many people of intelligence and integrity hold either one or other of these views, and these have been admissible so long as such ideas did not threaten the world with extinction. But now they may do that.

Censorship is a loaded word and has been argued almost out of existence with regard to the arts, but the arts never threaten to destroy the human race. Science does, and now especially, if, as I have argued, scientists might lead and save the world, they would need to think in terms of morality. A master must also be a servant. Science must come into line with the wishes of ordinary people. But the ordinary people, too, must find a morality to demand of their leaders.

If we are now to lead the world to safety, we must serve defined needs, but this time needs on the widest possible level. No one wants pointless restriction, but man must find some practical and acceptable morality which defines the furthest points at which we must say 'no' if we are going to survive. Too many scientific developments, from the H-bomb to the laboratory growth of human embryos to the prolongation of life in bodies in which the conscious minds are dead, are posing moral problems big enough to involve survival or destruction. Not to face up to defining a morality now will put mankind on a level with the concentration camp officials of the Second World War: 'It was not my job to think. I was only obeying orders.' If we did accept such a level of collective 'opting out', we should not deserve to survive, especially as, in this century, we have largely accepted that there are no 'orders'.

In the past, people looked to religion, and obviously there is some truth in all religions and great truths in most religions. Religions, though, in their widespread manifestations degenerate to the limited truths found through constant reinterpretations of the set statements or actions of some long-ago wise-man father-figure, and it seems to me that now the time has come when we, ourselves, must grow up. We must be our own saviours and leaders and parents – our own (perhaps quite literally) 'gods in the machine'. We must evolve our own wise truths and codes of behaviour, and since I also believe in doing something practical about my ideas, beyond just talking about them, I have devised a Hippocratic oath which would need to be taken by any scientist, technologist or engineer who did any work or made any decision that might have adverse consequences for mankind. This runs:

I vow to strive to apply my professional skills only to projects which, after conscientious examination, I believe to contribute to the goal of coexistence of all human beings in peace, human dignity and self-fulfilment.

I believe that this goal requires the provision of an adequate supply of the necessities of life (good food, air, water, clothing and housing, access to natural and man-made beauty), education and opportunities to enable each person to work out for himself his life objectives and to develop creativeness and skill in the use of the hands as well as the head.

I vow to struggle, through my work, to minimize danger, noise, strain or invasion of privacy of the individual, pollution of earth, air and water, destruction of natural beauty, mineral resources and wild life.

The repercussions of an invention are hard to foresee, of course. Lord Rutherford is reputed to have said that he hoped no one would find a use for radioactivity as it would take all the fun out of research; but the first practical application of his work was in the nuclear bomb. The invention of the car promised only usefulness and happiness to man, which indeed it has given; but people find in their cars a hideout, a status symbol, a sense of power often hard to reproduce in other aspects of their lives. No one foresaw, at its beginning, that when the car could give happiness to the greatest number of people it would also be self-destructive in blocking its own free progress, causing numerous accidents and poisoning the air.

But we can try. We can do our best to avert the dangers. We can do our best to bring about swiftly a time of peace and prosperity and freedom from nagging anxiety. Invention can be the power force that drives mankind forward through the opposing challenges/compensations of responsibility and achievement until we are big enough and bold enough as a race to choose and control our own fate: beginning perhaps with my Creative Society. Later – well, the achievement of the way of living I have outlined in this book might create a climate of Charles Reich's 'Consciousness' in which, with time to stand and stare, we shall become aware of something we like better.

What can, and must, be done

As Oscar Wilde wrote in his essay on *The Soul of Man under Socialism*:

a map of the world that does not include Utopia is not worth
even glancing at, for it leaves out the one country at which
humanity is always landing. And when humanity lands there,
it looks out, and seeing a better country, it sets sail. Progress is the
realization of Utopias.